One day in the spring of 1917, w[...] [...] across Western Europe, two Fokker triplanes of the German air force's Jagdstaffel Jasta 11 took off from their air base in France and headed for the skies above western Belgium, looking for Allied warplanes. One of the Fokkers was piloted by Captain Peter Waitzrik; the other by Captain Manfred von Richthofen, the famous "Red Baron."

Not long into their patrol, Waitzrik and von Richthofen spotted something in the sky ahead of them. It was not an enemy fighter. According to Waitzrik, it was a flying object about 125 feet in diameter, bright silver, and shaped like a saucer.

"We were terrified," Waitzrik said in an interview years later. "We had never seen anything like it. But the United States had just entered the war, so we assumed it was something they'd sent up."

Von Richthofen immediately opened fire on the object, hitting it.

"The thing went down like a rock," Waitzrik said. "It sheared off tree limbs as it crashed in the woods."

Waitzrik and von Richthofen then watched as two occupants climbed out of the strange craft and escaped into the woods.

"There's no doubt in my mind that it was no U.S. reconnaissance plane the Baron shot down that day. It was some kind of craft from another planet and those guys who ran off into the woods weren't Americans."

Though he went on to shoot down a total of eighty Allied planes, von Richthofen would be dead within a year. Waitzrik survived the Great War and the next one, and became an airline pilot.

About his encounter with the strange aerial craft, he confided years later: "Except for my wife and grandkids, I never told a soul."

UFOs IN WARTIME

What They Didn't Want You to Know

Mack Maloney

BERKLEY BOOKS, NEW YORK

THE BERKLEY PUBLISHING GROUP
Published by the Penguin Group
Penguin Group (USA) Inc.
375 Hudson Street, New York, New York 10014, USA
Penguin Group (Canada), 90 Eglinton Avenue East, Suite 700, Toronto, Ontario M4P 2Y3, Canada (a division of Pearson Penguin Canada Inc.)
Penguin Books Ltd., 80 Strand, London WC2R 0RL, England
Penguin Group Ireland, 25 St. Stephen's Green, Dublin 2, Ireland (a division of Penguin Books Ltd.)
Penguin Group (Australia), 250 Camberwell Road, Camberwell, Victoria 3124, Australia (a division of Pearson Australia Group Pty. Ltd.)
Penguin Books India Pvt. Ltd., 11 Community Centre, Panchsheel Park, New Delhi—110 017, India
Penguin Group (NZ), 67 Apollo Drive, Rosedale, Auckland 0632, New Zealand (a division of Pearson New Zealand Ltd.)
Penguin Books (South Africa) (Pty.) Ltd., 24 Sturdee Avenue, Rosebank, Johannesburg 2196, South Africa

Penguin Books Ltd., Registered Offices: 80 Strand, London WC2R 0RL, England

The publisher does not have any control over and does not assume any responsibility for author or third-party websites or their content.

UFOs IN WARTIME

A Berkley Book / published by arrangement with Kelcorp, Inc.

PRINTING HISTORY
Berkley mass-market edition / December 2011

Copyright © 2011 by Brian Kelleher.
Cover design by Pyrographx.

ISBN: 978-0-425-24011-3

BERKLEY®
Berkley Books are published by The Berkley Publishing Group,
a division of Penguin Group (USA) Inc.,
375 Hudson Street, New York, New York 10014.
BERKLEY® is a registered trademark of Penguin Group (USA) Inc.
The "B" design is a trademark of Penguin Group (USA) Inc.

PRINTED IN THE UNITED STATES OF AMERICA

10 9 8 7 6 5 4 3 2 1

Most Berkley Books are available at special quantity discounts for bulk purchases for sales, promotions, premiums, fund-raising, or educational use. Special books, or book excerpts, can also be created to fit specific needs.

For details, write: Special Markets, The Berkley Publishing Group, 375 Hudson Street, New York, New York 10014.

For my best friend

ACKNOWLEDGMENTS

Thanks to Warren Thompson, Erik Simonsen, Mike Machat, Larry Blumenthal and Walter Boyne for help with the photos. For their guidance, Keith Chester and Jerome Clark. Also Amanda Ng, Tom Colgan, Dominick Abel and Erica Varela. Music by Sky Club. Special thanks to Margaret MacDonald and Mike Dominic, www.paladinfreelance.blogspot.com.

Go to www.UFOsinWartime.com for more information

FOREWORD

I was happy to oblige when Mack Maloney asked me to write the foreword to his new book, *UFOs in Wartime*. Having written *Strange Company: Military Encounters with UFOs in WWII*, I was more than familiar with the subject. Covering the years 1933 through 1945, *Strange Company* is an effort focused on UFO sightings made in both the European and Pacific theaters during the Second World War. Mack's book, on the other hand, provides a much broader view of a phenomenon that's been reported during every major military conflict since the First World War.

These conflicts have filled the skies with man's aeronautical wonders, an ever-expanding array of airplanes, jets, rockets, drones, flares, and balloons. Natural and celestial phenomena also made appearances among this aerial war material. But something else has been reported in war-torn skies around the world as well—unconventional objects that defy all explanation. Some of these baffling objects seem to come straight from the annals of science fiction. What makes these observations so important is that in many cases they've been reported by highly trained military aviation personnel—people with great observational skills—during a time when their lives depended on accurate identification.

UFOs in Wartime provides a valuable work for both the casual reader and the student of unidentified flying objects. You'll revisit a number of important UFO cases that still remain perplexing as well as many being reported here at length for the first time. In this accounting of mysterious observations, you'll learn that while our aeronautical progress has advanced through the decades, unknown aerial objects were, and still are, being reported.

I applaud Mack's curiosity and willingness to explore such a controversial topic. While Mack does not claim to know what these sightings represent, one thing is for sure: *UFOs in Wartime* will ignite many questions and provide much fuel for thought.

Keith Chester
May 11, 2011

PART ONE

Early Sightings

1

In the Beginning

On October 28, 312, Roman emperor Constantine I and his army were advancing toward Rome to do battle with his archrival, Maxentius.

At stake was nothing less than control of the Roman Empire. Scribes traveling with Constantine reported that shortly before the momentous battle, a mysterious object appeared in the sky and hovered over the army. Glowing and shaped like a cross, it was seen by all, including Constantine. The emperor came to believe the object's appearance was a message that his men should paint the sign of the cross on their shields before they went into combat against Maxentius. Constantine so ordered his troops, and they went on to win the historic Battle of Milvian Bridge. As a result, Constantine not only became sole ruler of Rome, but he made Christianity, which previously had been outlawed, the official religion of the Roman Empire.

It's almost too overwhelming to contemplate, but what

would our world look like today had it not been for that mysterious object in the sky?

UFOs exist—we just don't know what they are yet.

Those wise words have been written other places before, but they are very true nonetheless.

What some believe to be UFOs are mentioned throughout the Bible. They can be found on ancient coins and in cave dwellers' art. Chinese history tells of soldiers soaring through the skies in fantastic airships, using fire-breathing dragons as their wingmen. The ancient scripts of India describe in detail incredible aerial machines big enough to be flying cities. Likenesses of UFOs can be found on stone carvings from Egypt to Mesopotamia to the great Mayan civilizations of Central America.

UFOs have always been with us—and they're still with us today. We make movies and TV shows about them. They appear in modern literature, comic books and video games. Museums and monuments are built in their honor. And they *are* mysterious. But that doesn't mean we don't know a few things about them.

They frequently appear at night, sometimes in groups, but mostly just as one or two. They can fly faster and maneuver unlike any man-made aerial machine. They are generally benign, though they may or may not abduct humans in order to see what makes us tick. And they seem to be able to come and go at will, anytime, anywhere.

But UFOs have also displayed another intriguing tendency: They have revealed themselves with alarming frequency during times of war and human conflict. Incredibly, there were reports of a UFO flying over Normandy on

D-Day, June 6, 1944. There are numerous accounts of UFOs, dubbed "foo fighters," being spotted by Allied and Axis pilots throughout World War II. World War I also had its share of UFO sightings and aerial visions. The Korean War produced a number of particularly bizarre episodes. During the 1950s and '60s, in the midst of the Cold War, America's skies seemed to be virtually raining UFOs. There are even outlandish stories of UFOs aiding George Washington in winning the American Revolution.

The numbers seem to show that UFO sightings spike in times of war, or what could be called imminent war, especially from the mid-twentieth century on. But what does this mean? Is it because there are more aircraft flying during modern-era wartime—bombers, fighter planes, transports— so there are more opportunities for people to see strange flying things?

Or is someone looking in on us? Watching us as we go to such great lengths to kill each other?

This book is a collection of exactly that: incidents in which UFOs have made their presence known at some of the most unusual times of conflict, frightening some, confusing and puzzling many more—but rarely if ever interfering, which might be the most tantalizing clue of all.

For the most part, the stories here are a recounting of episodes uncovered and researched by other people, many of whom have dedicated their lives to documenting and studying the mind-bending riddle of UFOs. This esteemed list includes Jerome Clark, Dr. Richard Haines, the late Dr. J. Allen Hynek, Bruce Maccabee, Captain Edward J. Ruppelt (a military man caught in the middle), Jacques Vallee, Stan Gordon, Timothy Good, Robert Hastings and Keith Chester, who literally wrote the book on foo fighters and dragged the start of the UFO era back to the early 1940s, where it belonged.

When this great mystery is finally solved, people will look back on these visionaries and say: We couldn't have done it without them.

Sightings from Ancient to Modern Times

332 B.C.

Constantine may not have been the only famous warrior to have strange flying objects affect the outcome of his military campaign.

The renowned radio commentator and UFO author Frank Edwards once related what some might consider a fanciful story about Alexander the Great having an unearthly encounter during his bid to conquer the known world in the fourth century B.C. *(See the accompanying reading list at the back of this book.)

Alexander's huge army had come to a strategic river crossing. The Macedonian mastermind had to swiftly move his forces across the waterway in order to continue his campaign. But just as he was about to ford the river, two strange craft suddenly appeared in the sky.

Alexander's own historian described the craft as shining silvery shields with fire spitting from their rims. As Alexander watched in horror, the strange craft dove repeatedly at his men, to the point where they, their horses and his war elephants became so panicked, they refused to cross the river.

A similar if even more bizarre incident was said to have happened to Alexander during the siege of Tyre in 332 B.C.

But this time the strange flying objects seemed sympathetic to Alexander's cause.

Located on an island off of present-day Lebanon, the Persian-controlled city of Tyre had incredibly thick walls and well-designed defenses. These had stymied Alexander's efforts to conquer it for months.

One day, the "flying shields" were back. Five of them suddenly appeared in the sky over Tyre. Once again, according to Edwards, after slowly circling the city and allowing soldiers on both sides to see them, one of the shields let out a lightning bolt that crumpled a large section of the wall protecting Tyre.

This breach was large enough for Alexander's men to push through and eventually capture the city.

1034 A.D.

Even a casual reader of UFO literature has to be familiar with the term "cigar-shaped object."

The "CSO" is among the most frequently reported of all UFO shapes, having been spotted with puzzling consistency throughout the centuries, and never more so than in times of war. Maybe it should be no surprise then that what's considered the first-ever printed pictorial representation of a UFO was of the ubiquitous cigar-shaped object.

In his book, *UFOs in Space: Anatomy of a Phenomenon*, the great UFO writer and researcher Jacques Vallee tells the story of an early typeset book called *Liber Chronicarum*. Printed in 1493, and now preserved in a museum at Verdun, France, it describes within its pages an incident that occurred in 1034 in which a cigar-shaped object was seen flying through the early evening European sky. According to the text, the object was first spotted heading south to east.

But then it was seen turning abruptly to the west and heading into the sunset.

The accompanying illustration shows the cigar-shaped object, flames around it, rocketing above the medieval countryside. The picture has baffled UFO researchers ever since. What could have inspired such a tale and such an illustration, if not an actual sighting?

1235

Jacques Vallee also writes about an incident in 1235 that might well have been the first time humans decided to *investigate* a UFO sighting.

It happened in Japan. One night, a high officer named General Yoritsume and his army were settling down in their camp when they spotted mysterious lights in the sky. The general and his troops watched in astonishment as these lights performed amazing aerobatic maneuvers, such as circling endlessly and flying in loops.

Baffled by the bizarre aerial display, General Yoritsume ordered a scientific investigation of what he'd just witnessed.

Giving simple and even simplistic explanations for UFOs would become an art form hundreds of years later. Those who practice it these days would have been proud of Yoritsume's scientists, for the explanation they gave the general oozed comfort and calm.

"The whole thing is completely natural," Yoritsume was told about the mystery lights. "It is only the wind making the stars sway."

Strangely, a half century before, a document detailing the sighting of another unusual object flashing across the night sky was written. According to Vallee, this time in his book,

Passport to Magonia, the document describes the object as a "flying earthenware vessel."

Or in other words, a "flying saucer."

1347

Things were bad in Western Europe during the years of 1347–50.

In this case, it wasn't warfare that brought death and misery. Rather, these were the years of the fearsome Black Death, the bubonic plague that swept over the Continent, killing, by some counts, more than 100 million people and changing civilization's cultural landscape for the next century and a half.

While conventional science tells us that the fierce pandemic was caused by bacteria carried by rat fleas, there were also persistent reports from the time of strange flying objects moving low through the sky, leaving a trail of suspicious vapor in their wake. Wherever and whenever these objects were seen, the plague would soon break out in that area.

Further reports from this horrible time describe mysterious figures, origins unknown, who dressed in black hoods and robes and used scythes to unexplainably kill livestock. These medieval "men in black" would later become associated with pending death. Today, they are better known as the Grim Reapers.

Other strange occurrences while the plague swept Europe included reports of "comets" flashing through the troubled night, strange animals washing up on European shores and many times, sounds like thunder being heard even when skies were clear.

MACK MALONEY

1492

On the night of October 12, 1492, a man named Pedro Gutierrez was serving as lookout on a three-masted ship nicknamed "the Galician." The man beside him was named Christoffa Corombo. They were gazing out on the dark horizon of the Atlantic Ocean, intently looking for something.

What they saw was a light glimmering at a great distance. It continually appeared and disappeared during the night. When visible, the two men saw it moving up and down and flashing sudden explosions of light and intensity.

The light captivated the two men, keeping their attention on the horizon. The man named Corombo was captain of the Galician. We know him today as Christopher Columbus and his ship by its official name: the *Santa Maria*.

And four hours after the strange light was first seen acting mysteriously in the sky, Columbus spotted land.

1561

At dawn on April 4, 1561, the citizens of Nuremberg, Germany, awoke to nothing less than a titanic air battle going on over their city.

Hundreds of witnesses saw a pair of large dark cylinders launching a variety of shapes variously described as black and blue spheres, red crosses and aerial disks. Then, once these objects were launched, they began fighting each other while hundreds watched—for more than an hour.

The incredible event was reported by the *Nuremberg Gazette*. Additionally, an artist named Hans Glaser did a woodcut of the scene depicting the frenzied battle.

As with the CSO depicted in the previously mentioned *Liber Chronicarum*, what could have spurred this newspaper story and woodcut if not a real event?

1777–78

What might be the strangest UFO story in U.S. military history—and there are many—is that George Washington may have encountered extraterrestrials during the dark days at Valley Forge.

According to the website book-of-thoth.com, this story comes from a Scottish researcher named Quentin Burde, who claims that in the winter of 1777–78, a tribe of Native Americans that Washington befriended while his exhausted, demoralized army was camped at Valley Forge was actually a group of green-skinned ETs.

Springing from a reinterpretation of papers supposedly written by Washington's military secretary, Burde says he found references to "hovering lodges" and a tribe called the Greenskins who lived in a glowing globe in the woods nearby, a globe that was "sometimes there and sometimes not."

The Greenskins, Burde claims, provided the Continental Army with military intelligence and reconnaissance, and possibly advanced technology that helped turn the tide of the war.

Burde is quick to add, though, that he believes Washington had no idea he was dealing with creatures from another planet.

Rather, according to Burde, the man who would go on to win the Revolutionary War and become the first president of the United States probably thought he was talking to a powerful Indian war chief or a medicine man proficient in the ways of magic.

Unbelievable? Maybe.

But as strange as this story may sound, even stranger things are yet to come.

PART TWO

World War I and the 1930s

2

Something Strange in the Air

The Scareships

As the story goes, one day in the spring of 1917, with World War I raging across Western Europe, two Fokker triplanes of the German air force's Jagdstaffel Jasta 11 took off from their base in occupied France and headed for the skies above Belgium. They were looking for Allied warplanes.

One of the Fokkers was piloted by Captain Peter Waitzrik; the other by Captain Manfred von Richthofen, the famous "Red Baron."

It was a clear morning, with few clouds and a bright blue sky. Von Richthofen was Germany's top fighter ace at the time. He'd already received the Blue Max, the country's highest military award, and within a month he would be leading his legendary Red Baron's Flying Circus.

Not long into their patrol, Waitzrik and von Richthofen spotted something in the sky ahead of them. It was not an enemy fighter. According to Waitzrik, it was a flying object more than 100 feet in diameter, bright silver in color and shaped like a saucer.

"We were terrified," Waitzrik told the British tabloid the *World Weekly News* years later. "We had never seen anything like it. But the United States had just entered the war, so we assumed it was something they'd sent up."

Von Richthofen immediately opened fire on the object, hitting it.

"The thing went down like a rock," Waitzrik said. "It sheared off tree limbs as it crashed in the woods."

Waitzrik and von Richthofen then watched as two occupants climbed out of the strange craft and escaped into the forest.

"The Baron and I gave a full report on the incident back at headquarters," Waitzrik said. "But they told us not to mention it ever again."

For years afterward, Waitzrik assumed the gleaming silver disk was some sort of Allied secret weapon—until the flying saucer craze of the late 1940s convinced him otherwise.

"That's when I realized this thing looked just like those saucer-shaped spaceships that everybody [started] seeing," Waitzrik said. "It's been over eighty years now, so what difference could it possibly make? But there's no doubt in my mind that it was no U.S. reconnaissance plane the Baron shot down that day. It was some kind of craft from another planet and those guys who ran off into the woods weren't Americans."

Though he went on to shoot down a total of eighty Allied planes, von Richthofen would be dead within a year. Waitzrik survived the Great War and the next one, and became an airline pilot.

About his encounter with the strange aerial craft, he confided years later: "Except for my wife and grandkids, I never told a soul."

Captain Waitzrik's famous companion was not the first combat pilot to shoot at a strange flying object during World War I. That had happened more than a year before. On January 31, 1916, British Royal Naval Air Service sublieutenant J. E. Morgan climbed into his BE2c fighter and took off from his base outside London. It was nighttime and Morgan was on the lookout for German zeppelins.

While the British would one day become astute at shooting down the enormous armed blimps by equipping their airplanes' machine guns with incendiary shells, that technological leap was still a year away. This winter night, Morgan was on a recon mission, a sort of crude early warning system, hoping to spot any German airships heading for London. What he found above the British capital, though, was something else entirely.

First documented in 1925, in a book by Captain Joseph Morris entitled *German Air Raids on Great Britain, 1914–1918*, Morgan had ascended about a mile above London when he saw a bizarre object flying slightly higher than him. He described it as having a row of lighted windows and looking something like a railway carriage with the blinds drawn.

Despite its weird appearance, Morgan was convinced he'd stumbled upon a German blimp about to attack London.

German zeppelins had bombed England for the first time in January 1915, helping to ignite history's first aerial conflict. But the timing for the world's first air raid had been unusual. As a rule, the Germans preferred flying their zeppelins when the weather was fairly warm, between March and September, because in winter months their blimp crews faced freezing and sometimes *deadly* temperatures flying high above the British Isles. So, for Morgan to encounter an authentic zeppelin over London in the middle of winter would have been a little peculiar.

The mysterious object was about 100 feet above him when Morgan first spotted it. Again, still thinking it was a German blimp, he drew the only weapon he had—his service pistol—and began firing at it.

Suddenly the object shot straight up at tremendous speed and disappeared into the night. The object rose *so* quickly, in fact, that Morgan thought his own plane was actually *losing* altitude. This disorientation forced him to crash-land in a marsh.

Morgan was not the only person to spot the weird flying object that night. Fifteen minutes after his encounter, another British pilot reported seeing something unusual caught in searchlights panning the skies above London. Others on the ground later said they'd seen the strange object as well.

Whatever happened, Sub-Lieutenant J. E. Morgan holds a particular distinction in UFO lore: He is considered the first person to shoot at an unidentified flying object from the air.

If it was a UFO, that is.

To understand what Sub-Lieutenant Morgan may or may not have seen over London that night, we have to go back seven years, to 1909.

In the spring of that year, people all over the British

Isles, particularly along England's east coast, began seeing strange things in the sky. So many of these mysterious flying objects were reported, it became known as the Great Airship Scare of 1909. The aerial intruders, whatever they were, were dubbed "scareships."

In a story related by many, but researched with particular levelheadedness by journalist and UFO writer David Clarke (see drdavidclarke.co.uk), it all started in the early morning on March 23 when a policeman on duty in Peterborough, a city located in East Anglia, thought he'd heard the sound of a car approaching in the dark. Police Constable Kettle soon realized, though, that the noise was coming from overhead. When he looked up, he saw an object about 1,000 feet above him moving at tremendous speed. The object was oblong and narrow, had a powerful light attached to it and was accompanied by a whirring sound. It was so large, the policeman said, it blotted out the stars. He watched in astonishment as it quickly vanished to the northwest.

Kettle told his fantastic story to the local Peterborough newspaper, and it was later picked up by the *Daily Mail* of London. But even though the newspaper claimed another Peterborough policeman had verified the constable's sighting, the incident was soon forgotten.

Only temporarily, though, because about six weeks later, there was a veritable deluge of airship sightings over East Anglia. Suddenly people were seeing Kettle's mysterious craft everywhere. *So* many reports came in, the British press decided to pursue the story aggressively. A media frenzy followed.

The *London Evening News* and the *Daily Express* in particular led the charge. They dispatched reporters to East Anglia where more witnesses to Kettle's original scareship sighting were found. From workers at a nearby train station, to farmers in Norfolk, to a crowd in Ipswich, they all claimed to have seen the same strange flying object the policeman saw back in March. All of them described the object as large and cigar shaped with powerful lights attached; all of them said it was able to fly against the wind and move at extremely high speed.

With each subsequent newspaper story, more reports poured in from other East Anglia towns such as Ely, Wisbech and Saxmundham and then places like Wingland, Woolpit and Orton. As the craze grew, so did the number of sightings. Suddenly it seemed like scareships were being seen all over England, including London, fueling belief there was more than just one. At its height, scareships were being reported from as far away as Belfast, Northern Ireland.

Theories abounded on what they might be. Some speculated the mysterious craft were the work of an eccentric English inventor, or that they were small gas balloons carrying lanterns sent aloft by pranksters just to rile people up. Or maybe they were even secret weapons belonging to the British military.

But most people believed the scareships were actually German zeppelins sent over England as spy ships.

Once more, the time frame has to be taken into account. Due to a series of secret treaties and a hunger for score settling over most of Europe, it was a foregone conclusion in 1909 that England and Germany would soon be at war. And because the British military was not prepared for such a conflict, some government officials actually *wanted* the scareships to be of German origin, so they'd have an excuse to beef up England's armed forces.

The zeppelin theory was flawed, though. While the natural explanation for what Constable Kettle saw that night would be a German blimp, as Germany was the world's leader in dirigible technology at the time, very few military-adapted zeppelins existed in 1909, never mind ones that could successfully navigate a 700-mile round-trip to and from the British Isles in the dead of night.

Then there was the speed factor. Even five years later, once war had broken out, a state-of-the-art military zeppelin could only manage 50 miles an hour. Such a speed does not jibe with Constable Kettle's account, or the accounts of hundreds of others, who saw the mysterious airships moving through the British skies with incredible quickness.

The *London Weekly Dispatch* did an experiment. One night, a scareship was reported over the East Anglia town of Stamford; twenty minutes later it was seen over the coastal town of Southend, nearly 70 miles away. By matching up the two reports, the newspaper determined the scareship would've had to have been traveling in excess of 200 miles per hour to make such a quick journey—much faster than the fastest airplanes of the day and many more times the speed of Germany's best zeppelin ever. Even modern blimps don't move much faster than 60 miles per hour, and that's under ideal conditions.

Many eyewitnesses also reported that the scareships carried bright searchlights. Any searchlight that could be described as "powerful" would have to be heavy and would also need some kind of power source. These would be weighty items to carry aboard a lighter-than-air ship.

Some experts at the time claimed that even if the Germans *did* have a blimp in 1909 capable of flying so far from home, the winds blowing over the English Channel throughout May 1909 were southwesterly, making a crossing by a zeppelin flying from mainland Europe suicidal at best.

Even more mysterious, there had been a similar, equally unexplained airship scare in the United States during the years of 1896–97. If a zeppelin would have a difficult time crossing the relatively narrow English Channel in 1909, how could one have possibly flown across the Atlantic twelve years earlier?

The *London Weekly Dispatch* also concluded that if the scareships were somehow of German manufacture and were sent to do reconnaissance in anticipation of a coming invasion and war, why would they do so at night with only the aid of a couple of bright lights? More importantly, why would they operate in such a way that so many people saw them? Hundreds of people spotted scareships in May 1909. Why weren't any attempts made to conceal their activities?

Hardly good spy work.

Another odd thing happened as scareship-mania swept 1909 England. This had to do with Constable Kettle's employers, the Peterborough Police.

Asked by a reporter what Kettle really saw, a Peterborough Police spokesman replied it was nothing more than a kite with a Chinese lantern attached to it. When asked what caused the "engine" sound Kettle heard when he spotted the object, the spokesperson claimed the noise was coming from a motor running all night at a local bakery. In other words, when confronted with one of their own claiming to see something strange in the sky, Kettle's bosses tried to discredit him by offering somewhat ludicrous explanations.

This is interesting because when the flying saucer craze hit the United States some forty years later, the U.S. military and the CIA also started a campaign to discredit anyone who reported seeing UFOs. But even more sinister are the stories that starting in the late 1940s, U.S. government agents actually tried to intimidate UFO witnesses into keeping quiet. These shadowy agents became known as the "MIB," the infamous men in black. How strange then that Great Britain's Airship Scare of 1909 had its own version of an MIB incident.

This episode began with a sighting on May 7 at a place called Clacton-on-Sea in Essex. That night, a local resident spotted a long, torpedo-shaped object flying high above his house. The aircraft was moving very fast and bore two bright lights. He watched it until it disappeared into the night.

The next morning the man found a curious object in the grass on the cliff near his residence. By his description, it looked like a soccer ball with a long steel bar running through it.

Word of the peculiar discovery got around quickly. Though the police and members of the local coast guard examined the object, they had no idea what it was. They asked the man to lock it away until someone from the British military was able to study it.

About two weeks later, the British military took possession of the object and, later on, claimed it was a sea buoy used for naval target practice. Just how a "sea buoy" wound up atop the cliffs of Clacton is still a mystery.

Before the military took the object, though, the resident

who originally found the "buoy" reported that two odd-looking men had materialized near his house and were seen combing the cliff nearby, as if looking for something.

The mystery men then searched the homeowner's barn and the area where he had kept the "buoy" before the military retrieved it. When the owner's house servant left to go out, the men confronted her, speaking to her in a strange language. She fled back into the house and the strange men disappeared.

This was the first of many reports of odd, foreign-looking individuals seen lurking in the area of scareship sightings. And while some suggested these strangers could have been German agents, possibly ones just as baffled by the scareships as the British, no one ever determined who they were.

So what were the scareships?

Just like the flying objects seen over America in 1896–97, and subsequent airship scares over Australia, Russia, Poland, Austria and Belgium in 1913, the sightings have never been explained.

Based on eyewitness accounts of speed, maneuvering and flight capability, though, what people were seeing over England in 1909 seems clearly beyond the technology of the time.

The last word on the scareships should go to the one person who might have held the key to the mystery. During the 1909 scare, a British newspaperman managed to ask Count Ferdinand Graf von Zeppelin himself what he thought the scareships were.

His response was: "I don't believe in ghosts."

What Happened at Mons?

For the British, tales of strange things in the sky did not end when World War I finally started in 1914.

Scareship sightings continued over England even as real zeppelins began bombing British cities. Accounts of airships doing bizarre things above the trenches of France were also reported even while the fighting raged below.

But probably the oddest aerial phenomena story to come out of that great conflict, at least on the British side, was that of the "Angels of Mons."

It begins on August 22, 1914, at the very start of the war. The German army was moving west through Belgium, seeking to overwhelm France. Standing in its way was the British Expeditionary Force.

The looming battle was not evenly matched. Though better trained and equipped, the British force numbered only about 80,000 men, while the Germans had fielded an army of more than 160,000.

The two sides collided near Mons, a village in western Belgium. It was the first clash between England and Germany in what would be a long and bloody war. After two days of brutal fighting, though, the outnumbered British managed to stop the German advance. The Germans had taken so many casualties, in fact, that they declared a temporary cease-fire, allowing the British force to withdraw.

News of this British "victory" sent reverberations throughout England. Recruitment soared and patriotic fever swept the nation. But with it came a strange account that the British army had had otherworldly assistance in "defeating" the Germans at Mons that day. And this help, depending on which account one believes, was either transported forward in time or came directly from heaven.

The story went that just as the Germans were about to crush the British force at Mons, to the astonishment of both sides, an army of ghostly archers appeared. These bowmen fired their arrows at the Germans, cutting down enough of them that the overwhelmed British army was able to declare victory. It was even said that many of the German soldiers killed during the battle had died of arrow wounds.

The story seems to have begun when a Welsh writer named Arthur Machen provided an article to a British newspaper based on accounts he'd read about the Battle of Mons. This narrative was the first to tell of the mysterious bowmen coming to the aid of the British and slaying thousands of Germans. But the newspaper didn't make it clear if the article was fiction or nonfiction, so many of its readers took it as fact. When a priest published a reprint of the article several months later, the story took on another life, reaching even more readers. Then, in April 1915, a magazine called the *Spiritualist* printed an account of the strange goings-on at Mons, and that's when the story of the ethereal archers spread throughout all Great Britain.

At the time, mid-spring 1915, the war wasn't going well for the British. Again, zeppelins, real ones, were bombing English cities, the *Lusitania* had just been sunk and the bloody meat grinder of trench warfare was running full bore along the western front. The First Battle of the Marne had cost more than 80,000 French and English lives. The first and second battles of Ypres, in which poison gas was used for the first time, cost Great Britain more than 300,000 casualties alone. The British population needed a propaganda boost. The "miracle" at Mons provided just the tonic.

The story's details changed throughout the many retellings. In one, the army of medieval-style bowmen suddenly appears, as if transported to the scene of the battle from an earlier time. But by other, more popular accounts, these warriors were actually angels—or the weirdest UFOs ever seen—appearing out of the sky to cut down the Germans. Some versions even included a mysterious luminous mist that also helped the British overwhelm their enemy. Mysterious fogs are not unknown to UFO sightings.

Such variations led to even more published accounts of battlefield visions occurring over the western front, including some that claimed Joan of Arc herself had appeared and aided the Allies in battle.

These newer stories became rampant in the latter half of 1915, with many being attributed to anonymous British officers whose names had to be withheld as a matter of security. For this reason, some saw the hand of British military intelligence at work, trying to lift the nation's spirits during a difficult time.

But while several investigations after the war found little firsthand evidence that anything extraordinary occurred during the opening battle of the Great War, the story of the heavenly warriors persists, suggesting it may never be clear what happened that bloody day at the village of Mons.

Miracle . . . or the Largest UFO Sighting Ever?

In March 1916, the formerly neutral country of Portugal was pulled into World War I.

Like almost all the participants in the Great War, long-standing treaties and secret deals had dragged the reluctant

Portuguese into the conflict, in this case almost two years after it began. Though the Iberian country was a close trading ally of Great Britain, Portugal's more immediate reason for joining the war was to thwart German designs on its colonies in Africa. Portuguese politicians felt the only way they could have a say at any future peace talks was to literally fight for a seat at the negotiating table.

Still, when Germany and Portugal finally declared war on each other, it was a very reluctant Portuguese military that formed the 30,000-man *Corpo Expedicionário Português*. Many in this expeditionary force were destined for the bloody trenches of France.

By the time the war was over two and a half years later, more than 2,000 of these Portuguese soldiers had been killed, 5,000 had been wounded and another 6,000 had been taken prisoner.

Coincidentally—or not—shortly after Portugal grudgingly went to war, three children from a small rural village about 60 miles north of Lisbon claimed to be visited by an angel.

This heavenly body appeared to them three times just outside the village of Fátima, telling them he was the Guardian Angel of Portugal. He urged them to pray for peace and prepare themselves for an even more fantastic vision sometime in the future.

About a year later, on May 13, 1917, the same three children were tending sheep in a small grove near their village when they claimed they saw a vision of the Virgin Mary. This apparition also urged them to pray for peace and an end to all war, promising to appear to them on the thirteenth of every month for the next six months.

Though the children had agreed among themselves to keep the incident a secret, word soon leaked out. A month later, on the thirteenth of June, about seventy people were in attendance in the small grove—but only the three children claimed to see the apparition. The number of spectators tripled for the July visitation, during which the apparition gave the three children a gloomy prediction of a world endlessly wracked with war and suffering.

The August visitation was delayed a bit when a local civil administrator, part of Portugal's solidly antireligious government, had the three children put in jail. Threats to the children to recant didn't work, though. They stood by their story, which only served to spread word of their visions even farther.

Though the August visitation took place six days later than prophesied and only in front of the children, there were 30,000 people on hand in the grove on September 13. As historians point out, this was an enormous crowd for rural Portugal.

But it was nothing compared to the October 13 vision. On that morning, 70,000 people were on hand! And many of them saw a truly amazing sight.

That day, October 13, dawned cloudy and rainy. But just before the time the apparition was expected, the precipitation suddenly stopped. Most of the clouds parted, leaving only a thin layer to cover the sun, just enough so it could be seen without hurting the eyes.

One of the children urged those gathered to look at the sun, and at this point, thousands in the crowd saw the sun begin to rotate and change colors. Many others saw it almost fall to the earth, coming so close it dried their rain-soaked clothes. Others saw it zigzagging. Some reports say the sun's bizarre movements were seen by people up to 40 miles away.

As fantastic as these reports were, a number of newspaper reporters were in the crowd—and even they swore these things happened.

One of these journalists was Avelino de Almeida, a reporter for Portugal's most influential newspaper, *O Século*. The newspaper was progovernment, meaning it was staunchly anticlerical. Still, in a generally accepted translation, Almeida reported the following: "Before the astonished eyes of the crowd, whose aspect was biblical as they stood bare-headed, eagerly searching the sky, the sun trembled, made sudden incredible movements outside all cosmic laws. The sun 'danced' according to the typical expression of the people."

A physician named Dr. Domingos Pinto Coelho was also on hand. Writing for a newspaper called *Ordem*, he reported: "The sun, at one moment surrounded with scarlet flame, at another aureoled in yellow and deep purple, seemed to be in an exceeding fast and whirling movement, at times appearing to be loosened from the sky and to be approaching the earth, strongly radiating heat."

A third reporter, representing the Lisbon newspaper *O Dia*, wrote: "The silver sun, enveloped in the same gauzy grey light, was seen to whirl and turn in the circle of broken clouds . . . The light turned a beautiful blue, as if it had come through the stained-glass windows of a cathedral, and spread itself over the people who knelt with outstretched hands. People wept and prayed with uncovered heads, in the presence of a miracle they had awaited. The seconds seemed like hours, so vivid were they."

So what really happened at Fátima?

As many ufologists have suggested, the answer may lie in subtracting the element of religion from the episode. Though the Portuguese government was virulently antireligious, the country's population itself was overwhelmingly Catholic. Had these events happened in a place that was decidedly more secular, with a citizenry more diverse in its religious beliefs, the story might read differently.

An otherworldly visitor contacts three children, telling them to prepare for another even more important cosmic visitor. This second visitor appears to them, as promised, on the same day of the month, for half a year. On the sixth and final visit, a massive crowd witnesses a colorful silver disk dancing across the sky, giving off sparks, coming so close to them, its heat can dry their clothes.

With a few tweaks, this description sounds not unlike many UFO reports—leading some to claim that the whole episode was actually one massive UFO sighting over a small country that was suffering relatively large casualties in a war it didn't want to fight in the first place.

Further proof may be found in claims that UFOs are still reported frequently around Fátima today.

3

The Ghost Fliers

It was one night in late November 1933 that residents across the expansive Västerbotten region of Sweden first realized something very unusual was making its way through their skies.

That night, an aircraft had been spotted twisting a path through Västerbotten's rugged mountain valleys. Flying almost suicidally low, with powerful searchlights hanging from its fuselage and its loud engine noise disrupting the Arctic landscape, the aircraft seemed to be heading westward, in the direction of Norway.

This was strange because in 1933 airplanes were still something of a novelty in this frozen, desolate part of the world. The few people who lived there might see an aircraft but once every few months, if that. So when this mystery craft appeared from nowhere, exhibiting such bizarre behavior as it flew across the 200-mile width of Västerbotten, the populace was very much mystified.

Local authorities were baffled, too. Late November in Västerbotten means the dead of winter and, this close to the North Pole, the middle of a long six-month night. Plus the region was battered by snowstorms almost daily, was frightfully cold, and blizzards were commonplace. Why would anyone be flying around up there if they didn't have to—and doing so in such a weird manner?

The mystery only deepened the next day when the authorities confirmed no border patrol planes or customs aircraft had been in the air the previous night. There were no military bases anywhere nearby, so the plane did not belong to the Swedish air force. The only explanation left was that airborne liquor smugglers were moving their wares from one location to another.

But then the next night it happened again. A mystery airplane was spotted for a second time flying over Västerbotten, its searchlights blazing, its engines roaring. The night after that, *more* mysterious aircraft were reported over the region—and the following night brought even more. But now reports of strange planes were coming from other parts of extreme northern Sweden—and within a week, people were hearing and seeing the mysterious aircraft not just over northern Sweden, but over Norway and Finland as well.

Thus began one of the strangest chapters in UFO history: the case of the Scandinavian ghost fliers.

The first person to get a really close look at one of the mystery planes was Olov Hedlund of Sorsele, Sweden.

Up to this point, the phantom aircraft had been spotted mostly from afar—shadows against the dark sky, as one witness had called them. The noise of their engines and the glow of their spotlights had attracted most of the attention.

But according to an article published in *UFO-Sweden News*, on New Year's Eve, just hours before 1934 was about to begin, Hedlund heard something going over his house. He looked outside to see a large airplane reflected in the moonlight. It was painted dull gray with no identification numbers or country insignia. Oddly, it was equipped with pontoons.

The ghostly craft was flying at about 1,200 feet, Hedlund said. Once it had passed over his house, it began circling a nearby railroad station, its engines making a huge racket. It did this for some time before finally veering off toward some railroad tracks and, almost as if it were following them, eventually disappeared to the north. Little did anyone know this sort of weird behavior would soon be repeated many times over.

The sightings continued throughout January 1934; there were more than two dozen reports of ghost fliers in those four weeks—and more frequently, the mysterious aircraft were observed doing very odd things.

The ghost planes were almost always seen displaying powerful searchlights. Many times, they were spotted, their beacons illuminated, circling a village, a railroad station or a mountaintop, bathing it in light.

The ghost planes were also somehow able to fly in all kinds of weather, including blizzards, conditions that would keep all other aircraft on the ground. And there were definitely more than just one aircraft. On some days, ghost fliers were reported in parts of southern *and* northern Sweden simultaneously.

Sometimes the ghost planes were even seen flying in formations. According to a series of articles written by the great UFO researcher John Keel for *Flying Saucer Review*, one resident of northern Sweden watched a trio of the aerial phantoms, aligned in a perfect triangle formation, fly past his house almost every night for three weeks. And the ghost planes were frequently spotted with pontoons, even though they were flying over an Arctic terrain in frigid winter weather, with little access to open water.

One truly bizarre antic of the ghost fliers was to sometimes turn off their engines while circling a village. In many cases, the residents would be outside looking up at the strange visitor and would hear the plane's engines suddenly stop, only to restart again a few seconds later.

The Swedish military, as well as the militaries of Norway and Finland, took all this very seriously. The combined Scandinavian air forces were in the skies every night, determined to find the ghost planes.

But though the three countries tried to concentrate their flights where sightings were being reported and were in constant contact with authorities on the ground, their searches always came up empty—at the cost of six Swedish air force planes that crashed during these search missions. And even though the ghost planes were observed flying fairly consistent flight paths at fairly consistent times of day, none of them was ever intercepted, or even spotted by the patrolling warplanes.

What were the ghost fliers?

Often in cases like this, it's easier to talk about what they were *not*.

While the reason for ghost fliers' bizarre activities remained unknown, there *were* theories about where they'd come from. Many people thought they were spy planes sent by Nazi Germany, just a few hundred miles to the south. One hypothesis said these spy planes were being launched from a top secret German aircraft carrier hidden somewhere in the Arctic Sea.

But this idea is flawed. Nazi Germany never had an operational aircraft carrier—and while it's not impossible that a German cruiser equipped to launch and retrieve floatplanes could have secluded itself in the frigid waters, operating aircraft from a ship at sea is difficult, even in the present day. Doing it in the Arctic, with its ice storms, high winds and impenetrable blizzards, would be a hugely complex and dangerous thing to do.

But even if the Germans *were* able to launch a dozen or more aircraft at sea, at night, in brutal subpolar conditions, doing it every day for what turned out to be many months would have been a titanic, grueling and expensive undertaking. And no matter how successful it was, eventually this mothership would have to sail back home and get resupplied and refueled, causing a huge gap in sightings of the ghost fliers. Yet no such gap exists.

Moreover, any secret vessel capable of launching and retrieving as many as a couple dozen planes would need a crew of at least several hundred men, probably many more. Yet none of these people, nor any of the phantom pilots themselves, ever came forward before, during or after World War II to confess that they'd been part of this massive ghost flier operation.

Could the ghost fliers have been operating from a secret land base, perhaps in Germany, or maybe even in Russia?

This, too, is unlikely. While the technology at the time might have allowed one or two planes from Russia or Germany to make one or two of these mysterious flights, harsh weather takes a toll on aircraft no matter what era they're from. Back in 1933, most airplanes were still made of canvas and wood and many had open cockpits. They were not known for durability, and they were certainly not built to fly in severe Arctic conditions, night after night, for weeks on end.

And if they were spy planes, what could they possibly have been looking for? The Arctic Circle region of Scandinavia is so isolated that even now it can barely boast more than one person per square mile. There is nothing there but snow, mountains and ice. Why undertake a massive spying operation over the same swath of territory, frequently using the same flight patterns, for weeks?

As for the aircraft of the time period, again, very few of them had the range, the fuel capacity, the navigational equipment or, again, the structural integrity needed to make these flights. Certainly no German or Russian planes of that era had these capabilities, nor did they, or any other country, have any aircraft that fit eyewitnesses' descriptions of large multiengine airplanes (one witness reported counting eight engines) equipped with pontoons.

Interestingly, the ghost fliers had a lot in common with a previous unexplained phenomena: the scareships of 1909.

Both the ghost fliers and the scareships seemed to make use of technologies that were before their time. Both were known for using powerful searchlights. Both were seen by hundreds of witnesses. Both were believed to be spy craft, but in neither case did they make any attempt to conceal themselves—again, one does not conduct spy missions with searchlights.

The ghost fliers share something else with the scareships. The phantom airships showed up in 1909—five years before World War I broke out. The ghost fliers were first seen up close in 1934—five years before World War II broke out.

Added altogether, what does it mean?

Or does it mean anything at all?

PART THREE

World War II

4

UFO Over Los Angeles

In the early morning hours of February 25, 1942, the city of Los Angeles was attacked by UFOs.

That might sound like the opening of a science fiction book or the first line from a movie script, but it actually happened—in front of *one million* witnesses.

Though lacking both the etherealness of the 1909 scare-ships and the inscrutable motives of the Scandinavian ghost fliers, at least one very large UFO appeared over Los Angeles at 3 A.M. that February morning, bathed in searchlights, bombarded by hundreds of artillery shells—and seen by at least half of the city's two million residents.

This sudden grand appearance triggered a citywide panic that wound up killing six people on the ground and causing millions of dollars in damage. But because Pearl Harbor had been bombed just two months before, many assumed the object was an enemy aircraft and that the continental United States was under attack, not by otherworldly visitors, but by the Japanese. That's why the UFO implications of the story did not get a very large play and why still today many Americans have no idea it even occurred.

What happened exactly?

Told many times in many places, with a particularly good account found on Rense.com, the story actually begins on February 24. U.S. naval intelligence had issued a warning during the day that a Japanese attack on Los Angeles could be expected within the next ten hours. The city was already tense. A large number of flares had been reported around the area's numerous defense plants that night. Blinking lights had been spotted, too. An alert was called around 7 P.M., only to be cancelled a few hours later.

But then, early on the morning of the twenty-fifth, radar picked up an unidentified target 120 miles west of LA, heading toward the city. Antiaircraft batteries were alerted at 2:15 A.M. and told to be ready to fire.

Radar placed the approaching target so close to the coast that at 2:21 A.M. the region's controller ordered a blackout. At 2:25 A.M., air raid sirens began blaring across Los Angeles, waking its two million residents. Antiaircraft batteries, many of them set in rings around those LA defense plants, trained their weapons skyward.

At 2:43 A.M. planes were reported over Long Beach. A few minutes later a coast artillery officer spotted about two dozen aircraft over Los Angeles itself. At 3:06 A.M., antiaircraft batteries all around the city began firing, and in the words of the U.S. Air Force's own history of the incident, "the air over Los Angeles erupted like a volcano."

Something was flying over LA. But what?

Different people saw different things. Included in the one million eyewitnesses were several newspaper reporters. Editor Peter Jenkins of the *Los Angeles Herald-Examiner* wrote that he saw a V formation of about twenty-five aircraft go overhead moving in the direction of Long Beach.

A reporter from the *Los Angeles Herald Express* saw the same objects. He insisted that several antiaircraft shells had struck one of them, and he was astonished the object was not shot down. Reporter Bill Henry of the *Los Angeles Times* confirmed that there seemed to be a number of direct hits on this particular object, but with no apparent effect.

Quoted in *Beyond Earth, Man's Contact with UFOs*, by Ralph Blum, who witnessed the incident as a young child, Long Beach police chief J. H. McClelland said: "I watched what was described as the second wave of planes from the roof of the Long Beach City Hall. An experienced Navy observer with powerful binoculars was with me and counted nine planes in the cone of the searchlight. He said they were silver in color. They passed from one battery of searchlights to another, and under fire from the antiaircraft guns, flew from the direction of Redondo Beach . . . toward Santa Ana."

One thing was for certain: These were not Americans flying over the city. Though the pilots of the nearby Fourth Interceptor Command had been alerted, no U.S. aircraft—fighter planes, bombers or blimps—were sent aloft that night, simply because the antiaircraft fire was so intense, the chance of a friendly aircraft being shot down was just too high.

Still, some people swore they saw dogfights between

enemy airplanes and U.S. fighter aircraft, though illumination rounds fired from antiaircraft guns were probably mistaken by some people for aerial combat. Others claimed they saw strings of red lights that looked like illuminated kites fluttering in the sky. Some people even theorized these lighted kites were launched by Japanese American saboteurs signaling the approaching enemy aircraft to guide them to their targets.

At least 1,400 antiaircraft rounds were fired over Los Angeles during the "battle," hitting nothing. Not a single bomb was dropped on the city and not a scrap of any aircraft was ever recovered. The only casualties were caused by unexploded ordnance that rained down on the area. This debris damaged many homes and cars throughout the city and killed three people. Three elderly residents also reportedly died of heart attacks during the incident.

At 4:14 A.M., the cease-fire order was given and the "Battle of Los Angeles" was over. But the controversy was just beginning, because at the height of the incident, an extraordinary flying object had been caught in a photograph taken by the *Los Angeles Times*.

And even to nonbelievers, its distinctive saucerlike profile looks a lot like a UFO.

As with the scareships and the ghost fliers, it's easy to determine what the object photographed over LA that night was *not*.

A Japanese aircraft? The answer is definitely no. At the time Japan did not have any aircraft carriers capable of sailing close to the United States, nor any airplanes able to reach California from Japan. Some speculated the object might have been a seaplane launched from a Japanese submarine lurking offshore. But the object caught by the *Los Angeles Times* photographer is definitely not a seaplane.

George C. Marshall, the army chief of staff at the time, wrote a memorandum to President Roosevelt after the incident in which he speculated that the "unidentified planes" might have been commercial aircraft flown over Los Angeles by Japanese agents. Why? To spread alarm among the city's residents. Other reasons for the Japanese to attempt such a brash plan: to pinpoint locations of the area's antiaircraft batteries and possibly to test the effectiveness of the city's blackout procedures.

And where would these commercial planes have flown from? The army speculated the Japanese might have a secret base in Mexico.

But this scenario was disproved at the end of the war when the Japanese divulged that they did not have any planes over the area at the time of the incident.

Could the object photographed over Los Angeles have been a blimp or a barrage balloon? The British used barrage balloons to ensnare low-flying enemy planes during the London Blitz. But while LA did have three of its own barrage balloons, they were all accounted for that night.

As UFO writer Frank Warren has pointed out, it's important to note that the object in the photograph is taking direct hits from antiaircraft fire. So, the question must be asked: What, in 1942, could achieve flight, was elliptical in shape, was silvery in color and could survive direct hits from three-inch antiaircraft guns?

All this eventually led to speculation that whatever was

flying over Los Angeles on February 25 was not of earthly origin—and the famous photo seems to bear this out. It shows an object of definite saucer shape caught in searchlights and surrounded by exploding antiaircraft shells. Physicist Bruce Maccabee, who wrote a detailed report about the LA incident, concluded that based on estimates of altitude and the spread of the searchlight beams, the object in the photo could have measured up to 300 feet across!

Whether the U.S. military had quick access to the *Los Angeles Times* photo is unknown. But the following day, Secretary of the Navy Frank Knox said the whole "LA Raid" incident was a false alarm, something that could be attributed to "jittery nerves." (Early 1942 *was* a nervous time for Southern Californians. Just the day before, a Japanese submarine had surfaced off the town of Goleta about an hour north of LA and fired on an oil refinery there.)

Yet many doubted Knox's explanation, including the U.S. Army, which later issued a statement saying *some kind* of aircraft were over Los Angeles that night.

The press was also skeptical. An editorial appearing in the *Long Beach Independent* soon after the incident stated, "There is a mysterious reticence about the whole affair and it appears that some form of censorship is trying to halt discussion on the matter."

There may be some truth to this. Until the release of that Marshall memorandum some thirty years later, the Defense Department claimed it had no record of the event. No congressional investigation was ever conducted, nor any reasonable explanation given by any government agency as to what happened.

Just about the only thing everyone agrees on is that in the predawn hours of February 25, 1942, something saucer-like and huge, something that couldn't be damaged by anti-aircraft fire, something that was seen by almost a million people, flew over the city of Los Angeles.

5

The Mystery
of the Foo Fighters

Someone Was Watching

It all began in either March or June 1942.

That no one knows the date for sure indicates on the grand scale of things how unimportant it seemed at the time.

Total war was raging around the world: Europe, North Africa and Asia were in flames. The Atlantic and the Pacific were killing zones. Millions of men were under arms; thousands of noncombatants were being slaughtered every day. The democracies against totalitarianism. Good versus evil. Freedom or slavery. This was World War II. And in 1942, the outcome was far from certain.

That spring, Germany was bombing Britain, and Britain was bombing Nazi-occupied Europe. The relentless two-way battle put numerous airplanes in the air, especially at night. Antiaircraft fire, bombs exploding, flaming debris, planes being shot down—it added up to a lot of confusion in the sky.

But among it all, riding on the same airstreams as the Heinkels and Messerschmitts flying west and the Wellingtons and Lancasters flying east, there was something else. Strange airborne things were seen by many: glowing green balls, luminous disks, cigar-shaped objects, weird flying craft—some of gigantic sizes—that displayed incredible speed, impossible maneuverability and for lack of a better explanation, a bizarre curiosity about what was going on in earth's war-torn skies. "Strange Company" is how UFO author Keith Chester so aptly described them in his outstanding book of the same name.

They would also become known as the "foo fighters."

The first detailed report of a foo fighter encounter came from Flight Lieutenant Roman Sabinski. A member of the 301 Squadron of a Polish division attached to the Royal Air Force (RAF), on either March 25 or June 25, 1942 (no exact report exists), Sabinski was flying a Wellington bomber over the Zuiderzee, off the coast of Holland. He and his crew were heading west, returning home from a bombing mission over Germany.

The flight had been routine until Sabinski's rear gunner called him on the plane's interphone. Some kind of flying object was approaching their plane from behind. Disk shaped and luminous, it seemed to be several miles away. Still, even at that distance it looked larger than the full moon.

Sabinski assumed the object was some type of enemy

aircraft, so he directed the rear gunner to open fire as soon as it came in range. When the strange disk got within 200 yards of Sabinski's aircraft, the gunner did just that. Firing both tracer and standard machine gun rounds, he hit the target, but—in shades of the strange flying object that had appeared over Los Angeles earlier that year—his barrage had no effect. The rounds simply disappeared once they struck the disk.

This went on for about two minutes—the gunner firing but with no results. Then the object zoomed ahead, taking up a position about 200 yards off the Wellington's left wing. Now both the front and rear machine gunners were firing at it. But again, the object seemed impervious to bullets.

Sabinski began a series of evasive maneuvers, trying to shake whatever this thing was. But the object kept pace with him, always staying in the same position relative to his aircraft. Finally Sabinski gave up trying to elude it. His gunners made one last attempt to destroy their pursuer, but this failed as well.

A few moments later, the object moved to a point in front of the Wellington, remained there briefly, then shot straight up at tremendous speed and disappeared.

Shaken by the strange encounter, Sabinski nevertheless managed to return to base, getting his crew and plane home safely. As was standard procedure, he was immediately debriefed by his unit's intelligence officer. But when the Polish pilot revealed what he'd seen, the intelligence officer's only response was to ask Sabinski if he'd been drinking.

Later on, Sabinski talked with other members of his squadron and discovered that the crew of a Wellington traveling behind his plane had seen the strange flying object, too. But, fearing the same kind of ridicule that Sabinski had endured, this crew had not reported it.

Thus began what would become regular sightings by Allied airmen of unexplained aerial objects, flying not just over war-torn Europe but in the Pacific theater as well. They would have many names until christened foo fighters two years later. "Unconventional aircraft." "Meteors." "Rockets." "Suspected secret weapons."

Whatever the label, though, and no matter how many attempts were made to explain the objects, they became a perplexing mystery, and in some cases, a dangerous distraction to the people who were in charge of winning the war.

There were scattered reports of similarly strange aerial encounters during the rest of 1942. British bomber crews witnessed weird lights over Aachen, Germany, on the night of August 11, then again over Osnabrück on August 17 and over the Somme in occupied France in December.

Then, in January 1943, U.S. bomber crews began reporting unusual aerial phenomena, too. On January 11, a B-17 crew saw something in the sky that one witness described as a smoke ball, and another as a swarm of bees.

Four days later, on January 15, during a U.S. raid over Cherbourg, France, several U.S. aircrews saw large numbers of projectiles—by one description resembling schools of flying fish—coming at them.

The intelligence officers of the bomber units reporting these things were baffled. Of course, the first thought was that the strange aerial objects were new German weapons, being thrown at Allied bomber formations—and indeed, the

Germans were always experimenting, at times somewhat desperately, with various kinds of new antiaircraft weapons, such as AA shells packed with loose shrapnel or even small glass globes containing the explosive thermite.

But unusual AA shells could not account for sightings of huge cylindrical disks, large "rockets" that turned on a dime, or gigantic cigar-shaped objects complete with portholes— again, descriptions that would be heard over and over from RAF and U.S. bomber crews as the war ground on.

Plus, of the many fantastic objects being reported by these same crews, none of them had shown any sort of aggression toward Allied airmen. No shots fired, no blowing up of Allied planes in flight, as would have happened if, as some Allied military people insisted, every strange flying thing encountered was a highly advanced Nazi wonder weapon.

So whatever these *really* strange objects were, they didn't appear hostile. But that didn't mean Allied intelligence officers weren't concerned about them—or how to report them and to whom.

"There was a lot of science fiction around before and during the war," *Strange Company* author Keith Chester told us in an interview. "Flash Gordon, Buck Rogers—that kind of stuff. When a crew would report one of these weird encounters, it put their squadron intelligence officers in an uneasy position. These men didn't want to write something in an intelligence report that would sound like crazy science fiction to someone higher up the command chain. But at the same time they couldn't ignore the fact that so many aircrews were seeing these things—and eventually, neither could the higher-ups."

There were hundreds of these encounters reported during the war. And because of the ridicule factor as experienced by

Lieutenant Sabinski, and again, the prevalent feeling among some in the Allied command structure that they just *had* to be some kind of German wizardry, undoubtedly many more incidents went unreported or misreported, being labeled as unusual antiaircraft fire and such.

So while the actual number will probably never be known, to those men who saw them, in both the European and Pacific theaters, foo fighters were real, they were mysterious, and a lot of times, they were frightening.

With special thanks to Keith Chester, Timothy Good, Jerome Clark and Lucius Farish, a list follows of some of the most unusual foo fighter episodes of the war.

The Ray Smith Incident

On the night of May 27, 1943, an RAF Halifax bomber was heading to Essen, Germany, as part of a massive bombing raid. Ray Smith of the Royal Canadian Air Force was at the controls.

Smith had no trouble finding his target. Essen had already been bombed earlier that evening; indeed, more than five hundred RAF planes would hit the heavily industrialized city this night. The fires created by the preceding wave of bombers had lit up the target area with a bright hellish glow.

Flying at nearly 19,000 feet, Smith's Halifax arrived over the target to find heavy antiaircraft fire being unleashed by the German defenders below. As he was preparing for his bombing run, and with AA fire exploding all around him, Smith suddenly noticed a strange object flying off to his left. It was huge! Long and cylindrical, and much bigger than his Halifax, the silver and gold object was moving through the flak-filled sky at the same speed and about the same altitude as the bomber.

Smith called out to his crew, and five of them spotted the object, too. Incredibly, they could all see portholes ringing the entity, rounded apertures evenly spaced along its length.

The astonished crewmembers watched the object for almost a minute before it abruptly sped away. Climbing at an impossibly high speed of 4,000 miles per hour, it disappeared into the stars overhead.

Smith managed to complete his bombing run and then turn for home. Landing safely at their base, the Halifax crew was debriefed by their squadron's intelligence officers. But whereas the crew was certain the intel men would be astonished by what had transpired, they were met with the opposite reaction. The intelligence officers seemed unimpressed by their fantastic story and steered the conversation toward other topics, like the amount of flak the bomber had encountered or how many enemy fighters the crew had seen. Smith and the others were left with the impression that the intelligence officers were intentionally downplaying the strange sighting.

This was no surprise. Evidence suggests that as early as 1943, Allied intelligence officers were sending somewhat sanitized details of "aerial phenomena" up to the higher authorities, while at the same time trying to keep the whole idea of these unknowns out of the minds of their aircrews, so they could concentrate on the matter at hand: beating the Nazis.

In other words, when it came to reporting these mysterious flying objects over Europe, a system of benign deception was already in place.

The Mysterious Silver Disks

The German city of Stuttgart was one of the most heavily defended targets of the European war.

Located in southwest Germany, the city housed factories capable of building engines for Hitler's combat aircraft and troop vehicles. Several key military bases were also located near the city. Most important, though, Stuttgart was one of the major hubs for Nazi Germany's railway system. For these reasons, the city was bombed more than fifty times during the war; as many as 850 bombers took part in some of these bombing raids, raining down tons of explosives on the place. Still, the Germans defended it almost to the end.

On September 6, 1943, more than 350 U.S. B-17s set out to attack the city. Though many had to turn back for various reasons, of those that actually made it over the target, 45 were shot down, catastrophic losses for the American Eighth Air Force.

The air battle over the city was chaotic and bloody as Messerschmitt and Focke-Wulf fighters relentlessly shot up the incoming B-17s and hundreds of AA guns fired up at them once they were over the target.

But in the midst of all this, something else had happened.

Just as the B-17s arrived over the city, two crews reported seeing hundreds of silver disks, the size of half-dollars, floating down from the sky above them. The witnesses said the objects descended in a tight cluster that moved unusually slowly. This cluster was reported to be as big as 75 feet long and 20 feet wide.

In the heat of the battle some witnesses thought they saw

some of the mysterious disks land on the wing of one B-17 and start it burning. But that plane didn't return from the disastrous raid, so this was impossible to verify.

What was for certain, at the time the strange disks appeared, was that there were no enemy aircraft above or anywhere near the American bombers.

So if the disks weren't dropped on the B-17s, where did they come from?

When a "Rocket" Isn't a Rocket

On the night of January 2, 1944, an RAF Mosquito night fighter operating over Germany had a strange encounter with an unidentified aerial object.

An extraordinarily fast airplane because it was made mostly of wood, this particular Mosquito was flying over the German town of Halberstadt when the pilot and his navigator saw what would be later described as a "rocket" following them. They reported the extraordinarily fast "rocket" overtook them, at one point turning 90 degrees to reach a course parallel with them. The crew watched this "rocket" for about a minute, until it finally disappeared.

This report was just one of many from Allied aircrews who'd spotted "rockets" while flying through Europe's war-ravaged skies. And for a time, "rockets" became one of the catchall phrases used by Allied intelligence to categorize all the mysterious flying objects being seen during combat. It was a safe word used in an attempt to "de-sci-fi" their reports to higher-ups.

But what this particular Mosquito crew encountered was no "rocket," at least not in the 1944 sense of the word. The same was true for all those other "rockets" Allied aircrews were reporting.

Just *what* they were, beyond simply another type of foo fighter, still remains a mystery. But how foo fighters became labeled as "rockets" at least for a while is an interesting story.

The Germans *were* working with rocket technology throughout the war; this was evidenced by the V-1 and V-2 vengeance weapons that would make their presence known by mid-1944.

But at no point did the Nazi war machine ever have a rocket that could find an aerial target in the night sky, fly up to it, get on a parallel course with it and make turns to stay with it, as many of these "rockets" were seen to do.

That kind of technology would require at the very least an elaborate guidance system (either internal or ground- or air-based), complex steering mechanisms built into the rocket fins and a massive fuel tank to allow such a "smart" object to stay airborne for long periods of time. Plus, if it *had* been some kind of German weapon, why didn't these "rockets" fulfill their missions and destroy Allied warplanes instead of just riding alongside them?

The Nazis did have an unusual rocketlike weapon called the Hs-293. It was basically a small, unmanned airplane powered by a liquid fuel motor with a warhead in its nose and a crude radio receiver as its guidance system. The weapon would be dropped from a specially adapted Heinkel He-111 bomber. By using a radio-control joystick, a weapons operator aboard the Heinkel would guide the Hs-293 to its target, usually Allied shipping.

The Allies were aware of this weapon, so when aircrews started seeing "rockets" approach their aircraft, turning to get on their tails or taking up positions alongside, for a while Allied intelligence considered they might be Hs-293s, or something similar.

But there was a problem with this theory. Just because the Hs-293 was a new technology, that didn't mean it was a workable technology. In fact, the weapon was difficult to handle, difficult to fire, and especially difficult to steer, and so it was essentially a case of eyeballing it several thousand feet down to its target.

And the Hs-293 *couldn't* fly on the level, turn sharply, fly in formation with another aircraft—or speed away at fantastic velocities, which was exactly what Allied aircrews encountering "rockets" were reporting.

But again, in the military-think of the time, these mystery objects *had* to be explained in some way. So one British intelligence group decided that what allied aircrews were seeing were indeed Hs-293-type devices either launched from an aircraft or dropped by parachute.

But how could these mystery rockets turn and maneuver so fantastically? The British came up with at least one head-scratching explanation: Defects in the rockets themselves were causing "erratic behavior."

Thus the extent to which some in Allied intelligence went to explain away the unexplainable.

A related incident halfway around the world lends a measure of credibility that something out of the ordinary was going on over war-torn Europe.

It happened in 1943, though the exact date is unknown.

A military training plane stationed at Long Beach, California, took off and climbed to 5,000 feet. Suddenly an unidentified aerial object appeared off in the distance. It was bright orange and was shaped like the fuselage of a typical aircraft, but without wings or propellers.

The object approached the training plane at high speed, made a radical turn and was very quickly flying in formation with it. The object stayed on this parallel course for about a half minute, astonishing the pilot and his student, before accelerating up to 5,000 miles per hour and disappearing.

Whether the Allied air commands in Europe had been made aware of this sighting is also unknown—but one thing is clear: The object seen that day off Long Beach was extremely similar in description to the "rockets" being reported over Europe.

Which presents a baffling question: If the aerial phenomena being seen by Allied airmen over Europe were being excused away as German "rockets," then how could almost the *exact* same kind of unidentified aerial object be seen off the coast of California?

Return of the Scareships?

By February 1944, RAF Bomber Command was pummeling Germany mercilessly.

On the night of February 19 alone, six major cities—including Munich, Stuttgart and Düsseldorf—were being bombed by waves of RAF aircraft.

In among the bomber streams coming and going in this brutal nighttime pounding, RAF crews saw many unidentified aerial objects.

During a raid on the Berlin area, two aircrews witnessed a glowing ball that came up from behind their airplanes at high speed, flying a steady horizontal course. In both cases the mystery object flew parallel to the aircraft before disappearing. The odd thing was that one crew saw this ball as orange red and the other saw it as pure white, meaning these crews must have seen two separate mystery objects.

But this was not the strangest thing to happen that night. Two RAF bomber crew, one taking part in a raid on Aachen, another near Coblenz, saw an object that both described as being silver and resembling an airship.

In one instance, this object flew a parallel course with the RAF bomber, same altitude, same heading, off its starboard wing. At one point this object fell behind the airplane, adjusted its course and then moved from the starboard side of the plane to the port side—an indication of some kind of intelligent control.

Five days later, on February 24, 1944, U.S. bombers were on their way to attack another heavily defended target: the city of Schweinfurt. Located in northern Bavaria, like Stuttgart, Schweinfurt was a crucial place for the Nazis because nearly all of the ball bearings for Germany's airplanes, ships, U-boats and tanks were made there.

The city had been bombed before, most notably on August 17, 1943, and then again on October 14. Combined, these raids cost the U.S. Eighth Air Force more than one hundred B-17s, enough to put an end to U.S. deep penetration raids for nearly six months.

Things had changed by February 1944, though. Where the raids of 1943 were conducted without fighter escort, leaving the big bombers very vulnerable to German fighters, by 1944, long-range P-51 Mustangs were able to stay with the bombers all the way to the target and all the way back, holding off those German fighters and significantly increasing the survival rate of U.S. bomber crews.

But during the February 24 bombing raid another strange incident took place. Three large silver objects were spotted below the main force of bombers. The U.S. crews who'd seen them were convinced they were zeppelins, even though the objects seemed to be moving in unison and not at the mercy of the wind.

If anyone made the connection between these weird aircraft and the scareships of 1909, it was not reported publicly.

But a larger question remains: It's extremely unlikely the Germans would send up three of their antique war blimps when they knew a huge allied bombing raid was on its way.

So, if they weren't zeppelins, what were they?

The Normandy Sightings

The Allies' massive invasion of Nazi-occupied France, famously known as D-Day, took place on June 6, 1944.

While the landings were costly in terms of lives lost and casualties suffered, they were ultimately successful. German forces were unable to push the Allied armies back into the sea or prevent them from establishing a permanent beachhead on the coast of Normandy. This foothold would be expanded gradually and serve as the starting point for the liberation of France and the Low Countries and the occupation of western Germany.

As was anticipated, the first day of the invasion was the

most chaotic and bloody. Hundreds of Allied ships sat off the Normandy beaches, some unleashing volleys from their deck guns while others delivered thousands of troops in smaller craft below.

One of these ships was the SS *George E. Badger*. A Liberty-type cargo vessel, it was positioned just off Omaha Beach, the scene of the worst fighting. Crewman Ed Breckel served as a gunner aboard the ship and had a front-row seat for the immense battle. Yet in the midst of all the confusion and gunfire, Breckel saw something very strange: a dark object, long and tubular, flying along just 15 feet above the water. Breckel said it was traveling on a steady circular course and in plain view. He could see no appendages on it, things an aircraft would have. But it was moving much too fast to be a blimp or a balloon.

Breckel had it in sight for at least three minutes before it finally got lost in the tumult of the battle onshore.

His would be the first of two unusual sightings over the Normandy battlefield.

The second came about a month and a half later.

Breaking out of Normandy had been no quick thing. The rough hedgerow-dominated terrain played in the Germans' favor, so the fighting just inland from the beaches was fierce for many weeks. It was late July before the Allies were finally able to push eastward into more open territory and battle the Germans on better terms.

George Todt, a columnist for the *Los Angeles Herald-Examiner*, was attached to a U.S. Army unit taking part in this breakout. One night Todt saw something streaking over Omaha Beach. He described the object as a pulsating red fireball. It was flying about a half mile high and made no noise.

Because the Germans had started launching their V-1 revenge rockets at England around mid-June, just after the D-Day landings, Todt at first assumed what he was looking at was a "buzz bomb."

There was a problem, though. The object was heading west to east, *toward* German lines. If it were a German weapon, it would have been going the other way.

Now with other people watching, including a lieutenant colonel, the object, which appeared to be several times larger than the largest star in the sky, slowed and came to a stop right above the nearby German-American lines.

And there it stayed, without moving, for almost fifteen minutes, before suddenly flying away again.

Both Sides Shooting ...

Strangely, there was an incident similar to the Todt sighting that same summer. But this one happened in Italy—and it wasn't so peaceful.

The Allies had invaded Italy in September 1943, their first assault on Hitler's Fortress Europe coming nine months before the D-Day landings in France. The Italian campaign had been a tough slog, however, as the Germans fought a brilliant defensive withdrawal, giving ground to the Allies only one inch at a time.

By June 1944, though, the Allied lines were well north of Rome, and approximately half of Italy was under their control.

One morning, near the battle lines close to Loreto, Italy,

an egg-shaped object suddenly appeared in the sky. It was described as metallic and glistening and reportedly went into a motionless hover over the front.

Allied antiaircraft batteries opened up on it right away, but then something even stranger happened: Nearby German batteries began shooting at it as well,

After a while, the Allied guns stopped firing because their shells were having no effect on the object. But the German gunners continued to pound away at it, even though it was unaffected by their AA fire, too.

Eventually the Germans ceased firing as well. The object stayed hanging in midair for a short while longer, then rocketed off at high speed and was gone.

The "Old Crow" Incident

The B-17 Flying Fortress was probably the most well-known bomber of World War II.

It was aptly named. Able to carry more than 8,000 pounds of bombs, it also boasted up to thirteen .50-caliber machine guns sticking out of both sides of the fuselage and its nose and tail, plus in turrets located on its belly and on top just behind the cockpit.

Enemy fighters would have to think twice about approaching such a heavily armed plane, especially when it was flying in the vast formations the U.S. Army Air Forces (USAAF) were able to send over Germany as the war progressed. When the U.S. military reached the point where it could routinely muster 500 B-17s for a bombing raid, that meant the Luftwaffe fighter pilots would have to contend with more than 6,000 machine guns while trying to shoot those bombers down. For the Americans, there was safety and firepower in numbers.

But some B-17s were called on for another kind of mission. Labeled a harassment raid, the USAAF would send up a single B-17 at night to drop its bombs on some unsuspecting German target; "unsuspecting" because in nearly all cases, B-17s only flew missions during the day.

These "Lone Wolf" raids were intended to keep the Germans off balance. So it was on this particular night in November 1944. Bad weather in the past few weeks had forced the vast armadas of B-17s, and those of its cousin, the B-24 Liberator, from bombing most of Nazi-occupied Europe. But in an effort to keep the pressure on, the USAAF *was* sending up Lone Wolf planes to bomb selected targets.

One crew, belonging to a B-17 nicknamed "Old Crow," had been given one of these solitary missions. Flying out of an airfield in Italy, their orders were to bomb a railway yard in Salzburg, Austria. According to the plane's pilot, Captain Bill Leet, he and his crew were briefed on their target preflight and told of what kind of German defenses they could expect—including AA guns on the ground and possibly some new German jet-powered night fighters in the air.

The "Old Crow" took off but quickly developed an engine problem that would prevent it from reaching its maximum bombing altitude of 30,000 feet. Instead, the plane could only get up to 18,000 feet.

This and other factors caused Leet and his crew to think it best not to bomb their primary target at Salzburg. Instead, they decided to go to their secondary objective, another railroad yard, this one located at Klagenfurt, Austria.

They reached the target area and were prepared for German resistance there, too, but then things got strange. Just as Leet was about to drop his bombs, his plane was suddenly bathed in a very strong light. This light was so intense the entire crew could feel its heat.

Assuming they'd been caught in German searchlights, Leet had no choice but to continue the bombing run. Once the bombs were gone, he hit his throttles, determined to get out of the area as quickly as possible.

What was so surprising was that Leet thought for sure they'd been spotted by the Germans—that's why they'd been bathed in the especially warm searchlights. But no AA fire was being shot at them. There were no night fighters around, either.

What they'd done had been almost too easy.

In any case, Leet turned the B-17 back toward Italy and headed for home.

But then a huge amber light suddenly appeared off their left wing. No one on the plane saw it coming—one moment, the sky was empty, and the next, it was there.

Leet described the object as being a perfect circle, almost *too* perfect. And it was luminous, he said, almost *too* luminous. Judging the size of objects at night is hard, especially at more than three miles high. But Leet guessed the perfectly round circle was about 10 feet in diameter.

Leet's crew wanted to shoot at it, but he ordered them not to. This thing wasn't showing any hostility, so he thought it was best that they appear nonhostile as well.

So they flew on, heading for home, their strange company flying right alongside them—for almost the next hour.

As Leet said later, the object's position never changed; its shape never altered. Its luminescence never lost its intensity.

As a result, Leet was able to study it clearly for a long time. He concluded that he could see no exhaust coming from it. And neither was this thing caused by an illusion or lights or exhaust from another airplane nearby. Leet became convinced the object was real but not man-made.

About fifty minutes after its appearance, the strange perfect circle suddenly blinked out.

Leet described it like someone flipping a switch. Just as before, one moment it was there, and the next it was gone.

The *Old Crow* finally landed and Leet was debriefed.

As was the case by now, whenever an intelligence officer heard that a crew had seen something strange in the sky, he tried to find an acceptable earthly explanation for it.

So as Leet said, when he first mentioned the luminous perfect circle, his intelligence officer replied it must have been a new secret German fighter.

When Leet disagreed, saying the object never shot at them or showed any hostility, the intelligence officer opined it was probably some kind of secret Nazi instrument that was sending back information on the B-17's position to German AA forces. But the mission had gone perfectly in that respect, too, Leet told the intelligence officer. There had been *no* German AA fire.

At that moment, Leet knew the intelligence officer had run out of the typical excuses for foo fighters.

So they were left with no explanation at all.

6

The Other Side
of the World

The mystery of the foo fighters was not confined to the conflict in Europe.

During the war years, strange unidentified flying things were seen over the Indian Ocean, over China, up near the Aleutian Islands and most importantly, all across the vast watery battleground of the South Pacific.

And while only a couple dozen unexplained sightings were officially reported during the Pacific war, author Keith Chester thinks the numbers are misleading. "The problem is, because of pressure from the Army Air Force to explain away these things, many sightings were identified by different names and placed under conventional categories," Chester told us. "Real unknown observations were mixed into categories of things that 'made sense,' like seeing a bright star, or a new secret Japanese weapon. Plus, many reports filed by the U.S. Navy have not been located yet." Chester's conclusion: "I feel there were probably just as many foo fighter observations reported in the Pacific as in the European theater."

So, while the actual number may never be known, there's no doubt whatever was happening in the skies a half a world away in Europe was also happening above Asia and the Pacific.

The Tromp Incident

February 1942, just two months after the Japanese attack on Pearl Harbor, the entire South Pacific was engulfed in war.

William Methorst was a crewmember of the Dutch cruiser RNN *Tromp*. The ship was sailing in the Timor Sea, close to New Guinea. Methorst was on watch.

As Methorst later told UFO writer Peter Norris in an interview, he was on the lookout for Japanese aircraft when he saw a huge saucer-shaped object about a mile high approaching his ship. It was moving at tremendous speed. As Methorst watched the object through binoculars, it abruptly slowed down and then began to circle the cruiser.

Methorst immediately informed the ship's bridge, but no one could identify the object, other than to say it was not any known aircraft.

Incredibly, the object circled the RNN *Tromp* for almost *four* hours, keeping pace with it and always maintaining the same altitude.

Then, unexpectedly, the object broke its orbit, accelerated to almost Mach 5 and was gone.

The Tasmania Sighting

A few months later, in the summer of 1942, a pilot for the Royal Australian Air Force (RAAF) was flying over Tasmania when he had an encounter with a mysterious object.

The RAAF pilot reported that the object was shaped like a large airfoil, about 150 feet long and 50 feet wide. The airfoil tapered to a fin at its rear, and the RAAF pilot could see sporadic green blue flashes emanating from this area.

The object was a bronze color, and on top there was a dome that seemed to be reflecting flashes of sunlight. The pilot theorized something might have been inside this dome wearing a helmet and that this was causing the reflections.

The object kept pace with the Australian plane for a few minutes before suddenly turning away. From this angle, the RAAF pilot could see four fins on the object's underside.

At this point, the object suddenly accelerated to tremendous speed and, according to the RAAF pilot, dove straight into the ocean. Buffeted by the Pacific waves, it created a massive whirlpool as it quickly disappeared below.

The Formation over Tulagi

On August 12, 1942, Sergeant Stephen Brickner of the U.S. Marines was sitting in a foxhole on the island of Tulagi in the Solomon Islands.

Located close to Guadalcanal, Tulagi had been firmly in Japanese hands until just a few days before. But a Marine landing on August 7 had lit off a battle for control of the island, a clash the Marines would eventually win. Later on, a U.S. Navy PT boat base would be built there, and among the PT boats assigned to it would be the famous PT 109, commanded by John F. Kennedy, who went on to be the thirty-fifth president of the United States.

But on this day, the fighting for control of the island was still going on. It was midmorning, and the Marines were cleaning their equipment in anticipation of more combat. Suddenly their unit's air raid siren began blaring.

Brickner slid deeper into his foxhole, ready for what the Marines were sure would be a Japanese air raid. Looking straight up into the bright tropical sky, Brickner recalled hearing the aerial formation before he could see it.

The sound was like a mighty roar echoing in the heavens, Brickner would say later. But this didn't seem right, because he'd heard Japanese planes before and this was definitely *not* the distinctive droning sound they usually made.

Then Brickner saw the formation—and was astonished.

Instead of the typical V shape that Japanese planes always flew in, what Brickner saw were waves of bright silvery objects flying very high overhead. Each wave was made up of at least a dozen objects, and there were lots of them—maybe 150 in all.

Brickner could detect no wings or tails on these objects, and they were going faster than any Japanese airplanes he'd ever seen. Though new to combat, and weary from battling the Japanese for the past five days, the scene still gave Brickner pause.

As quoted in Keith Chester's *Strange Company,* Brickner said: "All in all, it was the most awe-inspiring and yet frightening spectacle I've seen in my life."

What Flew Over Tarawa?

One of the bloodiest battles fought in America's war against Japan was for a tiny stretch of rock and sand called the Tarawa atoll.

Located in the central Pacific, Tarawa is part of the Gilbert chain, a string of islands strategically crucial to anyone wanting to control the thousands of square miles of ocean in that part of the war zone. Actually a couple dozen smaller islands grouped together, the Japanese had bombed Tarawa the day after Pearl Harbor and then occupied it a few months later.

Needing to secure bases to continue its island-hopping campaign toward Japan, the U.S. Marines carried out an amphibious landing on Tarawa on November 20, 1943. Eight brutal days later, 1,000 Americans and 5,000 Japanese lay dead, but the island was in U.S. hands.

By early 1944, a series of U.S. Navy radar stations had been built on Tarawa, allowing American forces to watch for any Japanese aircraft in the area.

In an incident related to UFO investigator Major Donald Keyhoe, one day in April of that year, a Navy radar man detected an unknown aircraft on his radar screen. The bogey was moving north to south at 700 miles per hour, a tremendous speed for 1944, and twice as fast as most of the U.S. fighter aircraft.

The news quickly brought a number of senior navy officers to the radar station. The first things they checked were the radar sets themselves, making sure they were working properly and that this wasn't some aberration. But the station's radar operators assured the brass everything was running correctly.

Then, almost as if to confirm this, a second bogey popped onto the screen. Moving just like the first, north to south, it was flying at the same incredible speed of 700 miles per hour.

At this point, there were only two possible explanations. Either the Japanese had suddenly invented a plane that had broken the sound barrier—highly unlikely—or it was "something else."

The two blips eventually left the radar screens, and their origin continued to be a mystery.

But the ending for this particular foo fighter episode was still about a year and a half away.

Mystery at Palmyra

One night in late June 1944, a Coast Guard vessel sailing about 800 miles southeast of Hawaii received an urgent radio message. A U.S. Navy patrol plane had crashed into the sea close to its location. The Coast Guard ship was asked to search for survivors.

Immediately changing course, the Coast Guard vessel rushed to the suspected crash area and used its searchlights to look for any wreckage or survivors. But they found nothing.

A day later, the ship was anchored at the nearby island of Palmyra. The ship's executive officer was on the bridge, standing watch, when he spotted a bright light over the island around midnight.

The light began to grow, even as he was watching it, coming closer with every second. For a moment, the XO thought this might be the lost patrol plane, inexplicably returning home. But on looking at the light through binoculars, the XO realized it was no typical aircraft, lost or otherwise.

It was a sphere, perfectly round, and very bright. It went into a hover above the Coast Guard ship, moving so slow that at times it appeared to be stopped in midair.

This went on for more than thirty minutes until the sphere finally picked up speed and moved off to the north, in the same direction as where the patrol plane had been lost.

The XO later had a conversation with a navy lieutenant concerning the missing plane and the otherworldly sphere.

The fact that the patrol plane had vanished was a huge mystery for everyone involved. Its crew was well trained and experienced. When flying over large areas of water, long-range pilots relied on their direction finder to be in working condition. But even if the lost plane's gear had malfunctioned, the pilots would have known which direction they were heading simply by noting the position of the setting sun.

As for the sphere, the navy officer told the XO that no U.S. planes had been up the night before and there wasn't a Japanese plane within 1,000 miles of the island. So whatever the XO saw, it didn't belong to either side.

As recounted later by UFO writers Jerome Clark and Lucius Farish, the XO admitted he believed the two incidents—the lost plane and the unearthly sphere—were related. The navy lieutenant had seconded that theory.

The missing plane was never found.

The Palembang Object

On August 10, 1944, a B-29 bomber based at Kharagpur, India, was on a mission over Palembang, Sumatra, bombing Japanese gas facilities in that part of enemy-occupied Indonesia.

The bomber was one of fifty flying the mission. This particular plane had dropped its bombs, and then, by releasing photo flash bombs, its crew began filming the destruction they'd wrought on the Japanese below.

Once their mission was complete, they turned back for their home base, flying at 14,000 feet. About a half hour into this return trip, though, two of the B-29's crewmembers spotted an oval-shaped object 1,500 feet off their right wing.

About six feet in diameter, the object's surface was very bright and pulsating vigorously. Its color was changing from intense red to orange, and it was spewing a blue green exhaust plume.

Thinking this was some kind of enemy device, the B-29 pilot put his plane through a series of extreme evasive maneuvers, all while flying at more than 200 miles per hour. Climbing, diving, turning, banking, the object stayed with the big plane through all of it, keeping pace and never missing a beat.

At the end of ten minutes of wild flying, the object finally broke off contact. Climbing straight up, it accelerated to tremendous speed and disappeared overhead.

7

Back to Europe

Tales of the 415th

Of all the American air units that served in the European theater of World War II, one in particular will be forever linked to the foo fighters phenomenon.

And while there is no way to tell for sure, quite possibly this unit ran into more foo fighters on a regular basis than any other during the war—which is very strange because the men of this unit were also the ones who gave the foo fighters their name.

The unit was the 415th Night Fighter Squadron. One of America's first ever night-fighting units, the 415th had been trained in Orlando, Florida, before being deployed overseas in 1943. They first went to North Africa, then to Italy, and finally, in 1944, they were stationed in France.

The squadron flew the Bristol Beaufighter, a British-built, two-engine, multiseat heavy fighter whose top speed was more than 300 miles per hour. And, because the plane was large enough to put a sizable radar set in its nose, as well as carry respectable loads of ammunition and fuel, the Beaufighter was a formidable night warrior.

The pilots who flew these night fighters were all above average in skill, daring . . . and eyesight. Theirs was a dangerous and almost foolish mission: prowling the night skies over Germany, like birds of prey looking for anything moving on the ground or in the air, at the same time they offered themselves up as tempting targets for German antiaircraft fire or their night-fighting counterparts in the Luftwaffe.

It took a very special pilot to fly for the 415th.

The strangeness started for the squadron on the night of November 26, 1944.

A lone 415th Beaufighter took off from the unit's home field near Dijon, France, and headed into Germany, hunting for enemy locomotives. After destroying a number of targets, the plane's pilot spotted a strange red light flying nearby. It came within a half mile of his aircraft before disappearing. As this didn't seem all that unusual at the time, the pilot reported the light during his debriefing and thought that was the end of it.

Until a few days later. The same pilot was airborne again, along with his radar operator and, this time, as an extra passenger, the 415th's intelligence officer, Captain Fred Ringwald. Because other pilots in the unit had reported seeing odd lights, too, Ringwald thought that if he was able to get a look at one, he might be able to tell if it was a new German weapon or not.

At some point during the patrol, the three men onboard

the Beaufighter spotted a line of lights a distance away. Ringwald thought they were lights on a hill, but they soon realized there were no hills in the area. Plus, the unit's ground radar people were telling them there were no other aircraft—friendly or not—in the area, either.

The three airmen counted eight lights, all in a line, burning bright orange. They could also tell that the lights were moving extremely fast.

The pilot steered toward them, but the lights abruptly blinked out. But then, just as suddenly, they reappeared, this time even farther off in the distance. The lights remained blazing for a few more minutes before diving very steeply and disappearing for good.

The Beaufighter eventually returned to base, but the pilot and radar man chose not to say anything about spotting the mysterious illuminations, fearing they'd be grounded with battle fatigue.

As for Captain Ringwald, who'd gone along on the ride specifically looking for mysterious objects, he didn't mention the lights to anyone, either. As Keith Chester says in his book *Strange Company*, the incident was just "too weird" for the intelligence officer to report.

But the *real* weirdness was yet to come.

A few weeks after this encounter, on December 16, more than a half million German soldiers smashed through the Ardennes Forest in Belgium, starting the largest engagement of the war. It would become known as the Battle of the Bulge.

Soon after the battle commenced, the 415th was back in the night skies over Germany, this time looking for truck convoys and forward enemy airfields—targets that, if destroyed, would slow down the Nazi onslaught.

One of the squadron's Beaufighters found itself over Breisach, Germany. Flying very low, its pilot spotted a half dozen red and green blinking lights aligned in the shape of a T. The pilot assumed they were enemy flak and kept on going. But ten minutes later, he saw the odd alignment again. This time it was closer to him and toward his rear.

The pilot turned left—the lights followed. He turned right, and the lights stayed with him again. No matter what he did, the mysterious lights followed him perfectly.

This went on for almost five minutes—until the lights suddenly blinked out.

A few days later: another mission, another sighting. One of the 415th planes was flying in the vicinity of Strasbourg, France, when its crew was suddenly aware of two large orange lights approaching them. They came right up to the Beaufighter, leveled off and then took up position on the night fighter's tail. They remained for about two minutes before suddenly turning away and then blinking out.

The next night: two more sightings. One 415th pilot on patrol reported seeing reddish flames in the air, at 10,000 feet; another saw a glowing red object shoot up toward his aircraft, turn over, then go into a dive before disappearing.

Two nights later: *four* more sightings. One Beaufighter crew saw two yellow streaks of flame flying even with them at about 3,000 feet. The same crew also saw several red balls of fire that flew level with them for at least ten seconds before disappearing. A second crew reported seeing four bright white lights, in vertical formation and staggered evenly, hovering motionless two miles above the ground. A third crew had a bright white light follow them for more than five minutes, despite taking evasive action.

By this time, it had become obvious that something very strange was going on. Almost all of the 415th's pilots had encountered the mysterious lights, and they continued to see them just about every time they went up.

It got to the point where the pilots felt they should give the mysterious lights a name. A pilot named Charlie Horne suggested "foo fighters"—from a then-popular comic strip called *Smokey Stover*. Stover was a zany firefighter whose fire truck was called the "Foo Mobile." (Perhaps connected to all this, the French word "feu" means "fire.")

In any case, from Horne's utterance, these strange lights, as well as all the weird aerial objects Allied aircrews had been encountering throughout the war, now had a name that continues to be used to this day.

Meanwhile, December dragged on and the Battle of the Bulge still raged. The 415th continued going up over Germany every night, looking as always for targets of opportunity. And the newly christened "foo fighters" were still continuing to dog them.

On December 27, there were two more sightings. One Beaufighter crew encountered strange lights throughout most of its patrol, describing them as bright orange balls hanging in the air, moving slowly and then suddenly disappearing in ones and twos. Another crew saw three sets of red and white lights, trailing them on both sides of their aircraft. Two nights later, on New Year's Eve, a Beaufighter crew saw a group of mysterious lights fly past them at 10,000 feet. The following night, more strange lights were seen over the enemy city of Strasbourg.

On and on it went. At the end of January 1945, with the Battle of the Bulge finally over and won by the Allies, the 415th's intelligence officer, Captain Ringwald, was asked to provide information on the strange lights his unit had been seeing. He prepared a report, noted in detail in Keith Chester's book *Strange Company*, that cited no less than fourteen separate incidents of 415th pilots seeing foo fighters while flying combat operations in barely five weeks' time.

And it didn't stop there. The 415th crews reported three more foo fighter sightings in just the first nine days of February.

Maybe it was no surprise then that shortly afterward, a group of mysterious men arrived at the 415th's base in France, intent on looking into the squadron's flood of foo fighter reports.

According to Chester, these men were not from any deployed location in the European theater—rather, they'd traveled straight to France from Washington DC.

They studiously ignored the 415th's commander, Major Harold Augspurger, and dealt instead with Captain Ringwald, the squadron's intelligence officer. These men then accompanied some of the 415th's crews on real missions, obviously hoping to spot foo fighters. But even Augspurger wasn't told whether the mysterious flying objects cooperated or not. And if a report was written about the shadowy group's visit, the 415th's CO never saw it.

The men left after just twenty-four hours, eventually heading back to Washington. To this day, just who they were, and who they worked for, is still a mystery.

Once Germany lost the Battle of the Bulge, the Nazi war machine was all but doomed.

Tough fighting continued throughout the winter of 1945, but by spring, Allied armies were overrunning Germany and Allied airplanes ruled its skies.

By May, it was over. Hitler was dead, and German soldiers were surrendering in droves.

Once the fighting had ceased, the dismantling of the German military began. This included the search for answers regarding rumored Nazi superweapons, including the foo fighters. Sightings of the strange aerial objects had dropped to zero since the German surrender, indicating to many that the foo fighters *were* indeed German secret weapons. But the U.S. intelligence investigation into Germany's arsenal, secret and otherwise, was just beginning and would take a while to complete.

This meant anyone who'd encountered foo fighters over Europe—especially those men of the 415th Night Fighter Squadron—would just have to wait for the official determination as to what they were.

This theme was borne out in *American Legion Magazine* in late 1945 in an article later researched by Keith Chester.

Written by Jo Chamberlin, the article reiterated that members of the 415th were anxious to see what army intelligence would find.

And if they found nothing? What if the strange flying things the 415th had been seeing *weren't* German in origin?

Then, Chamberlin so aptly concludes: "The men of the 415th will be all set for Section 8s—psychiatric discharges."

8

Back to the Pacific

The Sighting with Two Thousand Witnesses

The battleship USS *New York* had a storied history.

Its keel was laid down on September 11, 1911—an interesting date, considering what lay ahead for a future ship of the same name.

After doing convoy duty in the North Atlantic at the beginning of World War II, the *New York* was eventually refitted and sent to the South Pacific just in time to take part in the invasion of Iwo Jima in February 1945.

Once that action was successfully completed, the ship needed some further repair before its next mission, supporting the massive invasion of Okinawa in April 1945.

One day in March, between these actions, the huge ship was sailing near New Guinea, off the Admiralty Islands, when its radar room picked up an unidentified flying object heading its way.

The crew was called to its battle stations. Moments later, the bogey was spotted hovering right above the battleship, about four miles high. It appeared extremely shiny and silver in color. It was making no noise.

It is estimated that at least 2,000 sailors and marines aboard the battleship saw the strange object, including the ship's commanding officer, Captain K. C. Christian.

Two destroyers were escorting the USS *New York* at the time, and their crews saw the object as well. Everyone on hand was bewildered. This was not an airplane they were looking at, as it was keeping pace with the three-ship column, meaning it was making barely 12 knots. No plane could fly that slow and stay aloft.

Yet it was not a star, as it was daytime. Nor was it a balloon, because again, it was traveling at the exact same speed as the ship.

The only other explanation was that the object was a secret weapon fielded by the Japanese; that's why everyone was waiting for some kind of attack. But a half hour went by, and in that time, the object showed no hostile intent.

Still, its presence alone was posing a security risk to the three ships. So Captain Christian finally gave the order for his men to open fire.

Two of the *New York*'s three-inch antiaircraft guns blazed away at the thing, apparently hitting it. But the strange object appeared completely unaffected by the furious gunfire.

The barrage lasted long enough for Christian to realize his men were just wasting valuable ammunition. The CO finally gave the order to cease-fire.

Just as soon as the guns fell silent, the object accelerated to a tremendous speed and quickly disappeared, astonishing those hundreds watching below.

The USS *New York* went on to survive the war, and then incredibly to survive its role as a target ship in two atomic bomb tests off Bikini Atoll in 1946.

It was finally scuttled in 1948, but its namesake, the fifth ship to be christened USS *New York*, was commissioned in November 2009. Its hull was made with eight tons of steel recovered from the World Trade Center wreckage after the attacks of September 11—the same day, ninety years before, when the battleship *New York*'s keel was laid down.

Mystery Over Truk

On the night of May 2, 1945, eight B-24 Liberator bombers left their base in Guam and headed out on a night harassment raid targeting Japanese airfields.

While flying over the enemy-held Truk atoll—also known as the "Japanese Pearl Harbor" for its huge naval facilities—the crew of one B-24 was suddenly aware that two objects had sidled up to it in the night sky.

Flying at 11,000 feet, the same altitude as the B-24, these objects—one off the plane's left wing, the other off its right—were not only highly luminous, they were shifting their colors from red to orange to white and then fading out, only to reappear as red and start the process all over again.

The objects were riding just out of range of the Liberator's formidable collection of machine guns—ten in all—so the pilot began a series of evasive maneuvers to lose them. At one point, he dove as low as 3,000 feet, but to no avail. No matter what the pilot did, the objects mimicked his maneuvers perfectly and remained in place, pacing the big bomber. Even when the B-24 flew through a cloud, the mystery objects would lay on the speed and reappear ahead of the plane on the other side of the cloud formation.

After about an hour of this, one of the objects disappeared. But the second one remained close to the B-24 for the three-hour ride back to its base.

In this time, the night eventually turned to day, allowing the B-24 crew to get a good look at their strange companion. In the morning light, it appeared to be bright silver in color.

The bomber finally lost sight of the object as it was passing down through cloud cover, beginning its landing approach on Guam.

By the time the B-24 touched down, the object was gone.

The Mandel Sighting

Beginning on Easter Sunday, April 1, 1945, the Battle of Okinawa was the bloodiest fight of the entire Pacific campaign. More than 12,000 U.S. soldiers and marines were killed in the eighty-two-day battle; close to 100,000 Japanese also died in that time, plus a large number of Okinawan civilians.

Okinawa is so close to Japan—just a few hundred miles to the south—it was considered home territory for the Japanese, which is why their forces fought so hard to defend it.

Originally envisioned as a jumping-off point for the invasion of Japan itself, Okinawa did not have to play that role because shortly after the titanic battle for the island concluded, the United States dropped the atomic bombs on the Japanese cities of Hiroshima and Nagasaki and the Imperial government finally sued for peace.

Captain William Mandel was an artillery officer attached to the military government set up to preside over Okinawa after the fighting had ceased. His unit's bivouac was located on a bluff, looking west onto the East China Sea.

One evening, Mandel was atop this bluff, gazing out on the water, when he spotted a lighted object coming up from the south, flying about 200 feet above the water's surface. Because the bluff was about the same height, when the object passed by him Mandel was able to see it clearly and at eye level.

He described the object as being cigar shaped, about 30 to 40 feet long, with a diameter of 6 to 8 feet. The light that had first caught his attention was emanating from the tail of the object. He estimated the object's speed to be between 200 and 300 miles per hour. It had no wings, nor could he see portholes or windows.

It passed by him, flying smoothly through the night, making no noise. He watched it follow the coastline of the embattled island until it finally vanished from sight.

What's interesting about this sighting is the object's "cigar shape." Because it matched the same description as many foo fighters reported in the European theater, Captain Mandel might have had the best look of anyone at a CSO, possibly the most prolific unidentified aerial object of the war.

Up From the Ocean

Just like the Tasmania sighting in the summer of 1942, an intriguing clue as to where foo fighters *might* come from was revealed toward the end of the war—of all places, off the coast of Alaska.

It was summer 1945. A U.S. Army transport ship, the USAT *Delarof*, was heading back to Seattle after dropping off ammunition and supplies to ports in Alaska.

Sailing off the Aleutian island of Adak in the late afternoon, the ship's crew and passengers were startled to see a huge sphere rise out of the ocean about a mile away from them.

As more than a dozen people watched dumbstruck, the object went straight up for a few seconds then leveled off. Because it was positioned between the ship and the setting sun, the object's real color could not be discerned. The witnesses estimated the sphere was between 150 and 200 feet in diameter, however. And even though there were strong winds at the time, the object didn't seem affected by them, indicating it was self-propelled.

The sphere hovered for a short while—then it began to slowly circle the ship. The ship's guns were manned by this time, but no orders were given to fire at the sphere because it was not showing any hostility.

After it went around the ship three times, the sphere took off toward the south-southwest. The witnesses later reported they saw three bright flashes of light go off in that direction shortly after the sphere disappeared.

The ship's captain posted an extra watch for the trip home, in the event that the object returned. It didn't.

But once back in Seattle, fourteen of the crew signed a statement summarizing the incident and testifying that the sighting had indeed taken place.

The Galloping Ghosts of Nansei Shoto

The Nansei Shoto archipelago is located off the southern coast of Japan.

It's a strange part of the world, a patch of mostly water and a few volcanic islands, one being Okinawa. After sailing through it, though, many a sailor, including those in the U.S. Navy during and at the conclusion of World War II, became convinced this part of the Pacific was haunted by something, though no one was really sure what.

For instance, American submarines plying its waters would sometimes pick up sonar indications of ghostly ships that just weren't there. These things caused much consternation for the navy's silent service, especially operating so close to the Japanese Home Islands. A popular science magazine explained it this way: A submarine radar man would be monitoring his scope, his radar antenna riding just above the surface while the sub itself was riding just below. Suddenly the radar man would pick up an indication that something looking like a hostile vessel was heading for his submarine. If the radar man warned that a change in course was needed, the indication would turn exactly how the sub was turning.

The sub's captain would inevitably go up periscope and take the chance of scanning the sea surface for the opposing warship. But then, just as suddenly, the indication would vanish from the radar screen.

Thus the name "ghosts."

Many theories were put forth on what these things were—mirages, cold weather inversions, "air sandwiches," which are a freakish condition caused when low-lying cold air traps radar signals. But no satisfactory explanation has ever been proven.

Plus these spirits didn't just spook submarines. The so-called Galloping Ghosts of Nansei Shoto also shadowed the U.S. surface fleet. They were especially troublesome to aircraft carriers. On many occasions, night fighters would be scrambled to intercept the ghostly electronic indications, but no plane ever got close enough to engage what was showing up on the radar screen.

In the summer of 1945 a radar operator on an aircraft carrier steaming near the Nansei Shoto archipelago saw a "very large plot" suddenly appear on his radar screen. Incredibly, it looked like *three hundred* unidentified aircraft were heading for the carrier. Even crazier, this mass of aircraft seemed to be traveling at nearly 700 miles per hour—much faster than any airplane could go in 1945.

Navy fighters were immediately scrambled—and this is where it got *really* weird.

About sixty-five miles away from the carrier, the very large plot of targets began morphing into what were later described as "tentacles." The radar screen showed these tentacles wrapping themselves around the carrier!

The two fighters were madly flying toward the target; the entire task force waited apprehensively below.

But when the fighters reached the point indicated on the radar, they found nothing. The large plot had simply disappeared.

No explanation has ever been given for the strange occurrence.

The Stringfield Incident

On August 28, almost two weeks after the Japanese surrendered, ending World War II, an American C-46 cargo plane landed at Atsugi airfield near Yokahama, Japan. About 150 U.S. soldiers were aboard, the vanguard of a large American force that would soon occupy and govern the defeated country for the next several years.

But something strange had happened to the C-46 on its way to this historical landing.

The plane was flying close to the island of Iwo Jima when its portside engine began to fail. The propeller was sputtering oil and the plane started losing altitude.

One person aboard was Sergeant Leonard Stringfield, a member of the advance intelligence team from the Fifth Air Force.

As the airplane started to fall and all attention was drawn to the suddenly ailing left-side engine, Stringfield happened to look out the right-side window—and saw something amazing.

There were three teardrop-shaped objects riding in formation right next to the stricken C-46, matching its speed perfectly.

Stringfield would later say that he knew these were not U.S or Japanese aircraft. They had no wings, no fuselage. In fact, there was little evidence of any kind of mass at all behind the balls of bright light.

Stringfield kept the objects in sight for about half a minute before they disappeared into the clouds. An instant later, the plane's ailing engine suddenly came back to life. It was soon turning normally again, and the plane landed at Iwo Jima with no further problems.

Though it turned out that Stringfield was the only person on the airplane to see the objects, he was convinced they had something to do with the engine's malfunction and its somewhat miraculous recovery.

And while he was never able to question the C-46 pilots about it directly, Stringfield did hear later that during the incident, the plane's magnetic navigation gear had gone "crazy."

This episode had such an effect on Leonard Stringfield that after the war, he became a noted ufologist, wrote two books on the subject and devoted much time trying to get answers to the perplexing foo fighter question as well as the phenomenon's later incarnations.

9

What Did They Know?

What did the Germans and the Japanese know about the
foo fighters?

Next to "Where did they come from?" this might be the
most asked question relating to the phenomenon. Unfortunately there's not a lot of information to formulate a good
answer.

But there are some clues.

When the war finally ended, U.S. Navy intelligence officers had a chance to debrief the top admirals of the Imperial Japanese Navy. The United States was curious about
many issues concerning how the Imperial Forces had pros-
ecuted the war. These included any secret weapons the
Japanese might have fielded that the United States hadn't
known about.

Specifically, the U.S. Navy interrogators asked the high
Japanese officers about the "supersonic planes" that had

flown over Tarawa that day in April 1944, the incident that caused so much anxiety for the navy at the time.

The Japanese admirals replied, truthfully, that they had no idea what the navy was talking about.

There are other tantalizing bits of information concerning what the foo fighters were—and what they were not. But some clues don't rate high on the credibility scale.

As first reported by French UFO writer Henry Durrant, one story goes that far from being the brains behind the foo fighters, the Germans became enormously puzzled by them after their own pilots started seeing weird things in the sky. To investigate the phenomenon, the Luftwaffe set up a shadowy unit called "Sonderburo 13."

According to Durrant, Sonderburo 13's first case came from 1942, based on claims by a Luftwaffe pilot named Hauptmann Fischer. Fischer had been transferred to a secret Luftwaffe base in Norway called Banak. Just minutes after arriving, a mysterious object was picked up on the base's radar. Fischer was asked to go aloft and intercept it.

Climbing two miles above the base, Fischer found what he described as a *"Luftwal"*—as in "flying whale." The object was huge and streamlined, 300 feet long and 50 feet in diameter. It flew along horizontally just long enough for Fischer to get a good look at it before it took off, straight up, vanishing high above in a blazing burst of speed.

Though Fischer reported exactly what he'd seen, adding he didn't believe the object was of this earth, the Luftwaffe apparently thought he'd gone mad, the result of him being sent to such a cold, isolated northern climate; this was the Nazi equivalent of asking him if he'd been drinking.

Another incident that Sonderburo 13 investigated was said to have occurred on February 12, 1944, at the Kummersdorf rocket test center. A group of the Nazi hierarchy, including SS leader Heinrich Himmler and Nazi propaganda chief Josef Goebbels, were on hand to watch an experimental rocket being launched.

The launch was filmed, and as the story goes, when the film was processed, "a spherical body" was seen following the experimental rocket as it rose into the heavens. The Nazi leadership was convinced the unknown object was an Allied secret weapon. But then Himmler was supposed to have been told that similarly strange objects had been plaguing the Allies as well, and that the British in particular were convinced they were new *German* weapons.

The third major case that Sonderburo 13 was said to investigate happened in September 1944. A German test pilot, aloft in a Me-262 jet fighter, suddenly became aware of a pair of bright lights off his starboard wing. He hit the throttles and turned toward the lights only to find a huge cylindrical object, more than 300 feet long with an antenna on top, flying away from him.

The German jet pilot tried to draw closer, but the object was moving at the then-unheard-of speed of 1,200 miles per hour and quickly left him behind.

If true, the story of Sonderburo 13 would have answered a lot of questions about the foo fighters.

But there's a chance that the whole story of Sonderburo 13 is a fake.

Some years later, Henry Durrant, the man who first reported the events of Sonderburo 13 in his 1970 work, *The*

Black Book of Flying Saucers, claimed he'd invented it all just to catch UFO researchers who weren't checking their facts adequately. To this day, though, the story of Sonderburo 13 still perpetuates in UFO books and online sites.

This underscores just how difficult it is to get to the bottom of the foo fighter mystery.

There *are* some concrete facts about the foo fighters, though; truths that cannot be disputed.

It is no secret that the Germans did design and field "wonder weapons" during the war, the aforementioned V-1 and V-2 vengeance weapons, the He-193 guided bomb, the Me-163 rocket plane and the Me-262 jet fighter among them.

But postwar investigations of the defeated German war machine, including both document searches and searches of war material research facilities, revealed the Nazis had nothing even remotely close to matching the foo fighters' otherworldly abilities. So bring on the straitjackets for the 415th Night Fighter Squadron: The foo fighters *were not* German superweapons.

Furthermore, the myriad objects that came to be known as foo fighters—the balls of fire, the perfectly round spheres, the highly maneuverable "rockets" and the cigar-shaped objects with portholes—were seen in both European *and* Asian war zones. And, in fact, they are being seen still, in all parts of the world.

This *really* begs a question of anyone who doubts the existence of unidentified aerial phenomenon: There's always the possibility that someone claiming to see a cigar-shaped object with rows of windows on a darkened night outside his home might be accused of a leap of imagination or a downright hoax. But why would a crewman aboard a warplane in the midst of mortal combat make such a claim?

More questions: With all the evidence concerning foo fighters presented them during the war, why didn't the Allies do more to look into what was happening?

Two reasons. First, it seems many in the upper echelons of Allied authority were convinced, to the very end, that no matter how crazy the reports were, the things being seen by their aircrews *had* to be secret enemy weapons. But more important, those same upper echelons of Allied authority were not in the business of studying strange aerial phenomenon. They were concerned about only one thing: winning the war. Unless these strange flying things turned aggressive and started blasting Allied bombers out of the sky, they just couldn't be a big concern.

But what were the foo fighters doing? Chasing aircraft, pacing aircraft, appearing and disappearing at will? Obviously no one knows for sure—but maybe a more earthbound example could offer a theory. Israel and the Arab nations have fought several wars over the past sixty years. To varying degrees during all of them, the U.S. military kept tabs on the combatants and monitored major battles and troop movements and so on, collecting intelligence on both sides through the use of spy ships, satellites and high-flying spy planes like the U-2 and the SR-71 Blackbird. Is that what the foo fighters were doing during World War II? Acting as third-party witnesses to a war? Studying us as one might study two gladiators locked in combat?

It doesn't seem unreasonable—but it brings up another question: If these strange flying objects had such fantastic abilities, to fly the way they did, to move at such incredible speeds and to vanish at will, why would they come here to earth to do something so pedestrian as "reconning" our worldwide conflict? We can see billions of miles into space courtesy of the Hubble Space Telescope; why would an intelligence so advanced that it could build the foo fighters choose to use its magnificent technology to watch us so up close and personal and in such mundane ways?

As many researchers have found out, when it comes to the foo fighters, the more questions that are answered, the more questions that need to be asked.

There is emerging proof, though, that not everyone high up in the World War II Allied command structure believed that foo fighters were of earthly manufacture.

Subsequently released documents claim that in fact Winston Churchill himself was aware of the phenomenon and even sought to cover it up.

The story goes that the grandson of one of Churchill's personal bodyguards wrote to the British Ministry of Defence in 1999 looking for further details of an incident his grandfather had told him about.

It was claimed Churchill had been briefed during the war on a foo fighter episode involving an RAF reconnaissance plane that had been followed by a mysterious metallic object during a flight along the English coast. Photos were even taken of the object. At some point after the briefing, and after a British weapons expert explained to him that whatever the object was, it was totally beyond any imagined capabilities of the time, Churchill ordered all news of the incident be kept secret for at least fifty years.

Why? Because the wartime prime minister didn't want to cause worldwide alarm.

As quoted in the British newspaper, *The Telegraph* (on August 5, 2010) Churchill said: "This event should be immediately classified since it would create mass panic among the general population and destroy one's belief in the Church."

But while Churchill seemed to pick his words carefully, one of his top military men chose to be more blunt: "More than 10,000 sightings have been reported [during the war], the majority of which cannot be accounted for by any scientific explanation, e.g., that they are hallucinations, the effects of light refraction, meteors, wheels falling from aeroplanes, and the like. They have been tracked on radar screens and the observed speeds have been as great as 9,000 miles per hour. I am convinced that these objects do exist and they are not manufactured by any nation on earth. I can therefore see no alternative to accepting the theory that they come from an extraterrestrial source."

That quote was given to the British newspaper, the *Sunday Dispatch,* on July 11, 1954. The man speaking? No less than Air Chief Marshall Lord Dowding, the commanding officer of RAF during the Battle of Britain.

Maybe the most interesting quote on the topic of foo fighters, though, came from someone who unintentionally found himself very close to the phenomenon.

Again, as author Keith Chester points out, just like many people in Allied command, members of the 415th Night Fighter Squadron at the time believed that once the war was over, it would be revealed the foo fighters were secret German weapons. Yet again, nothing like that was ever found.

And while none of 415th members ever wound up getting those Section 8s, more than fifty years later, none other than Major Harold Augspurger, the commanding officer for the 415th Night Fighter Squadron, confided to Chester that he now believes foo fighters were indeed extraterrestrial.

"I think they [were] something from outer space," he told the author in an interview. ". . . Probably came down to Earth to see what the heck was going on."

Yet, claims that the foo fighters were of German origin, along with many other fantastic yet unseen Nazi weapons, still persist. Some ufologists consider this just another way to continue the myth that the Nazis were technological gods, and thus just another way of perpetuating the vile policies of the Third Reich.

But, for any die-hard believers in the Nazi superman theory, the same questions asked regarding the ghost fliers of ten years before must be asked again. If the Nazis were responsible for the foo fighters and the wide array of aerial superweapons still credited to them by some, where was the massive support system that would be required to build and launch such sophisticated vehicles? Where were the resources for the people running such a huge, extremely secret operation? Why was nothing ever found after the war detailing what would have had to have been a colossal venture, something that would have dwarfed America's Manhattan Project many times over? Why did no former Reich scientists come forward after the war to confess their involvement in designing or manufacturing such mind-boggling Nazi superweapons? Many of those same scientists emigrated to the United States in 1945 and helped NASA put an American on the moon. Why would all of them keep the secrets of such advanced technology from their new employers?

How could a cash-strapped, resource-poor Germany afford to maintain such a program, especially in the last year or so of the war? Where would they get the materials to build these superweapons when toward the end they were building their Me-262 cockpits out of wood?

Most importantly, and asked here again, when these fantastic weapons were able to get so close to Allied bombers, why did they never shoot at them? And why weren't they knocking down Allied fighters or immolating ground troops for that matter? What kind of "weapons" were they?

And lastly, if the Nazis had such sophisticated, stunning technology at their disposal from 1939 through 1945, why did they lose the war?

PART FOUR

The Postwar and the Mystery in America's Skies

10

The Ghost Rockets

What could it be about the northern reaches of Scandinavia that attracts unexplained aerial phenomena? Perhaps this is one of the biggest UFO mysteries of all.

No sooner had World War II ended, taking with it the baffling episode of the foo fighters, than once again unidentified aerial objects began showing up over the Scandinavian Arctic.

The unexplained intruders weren't ghostly airplanes this time, but strange rockets seen streaking across the skies of Sweden, Norway and Finland. As with the ghost fliers of 1934, many people saw them, including military pilots this time. They appeared almost always in the daytime, and on some days, literally hundreds were reported.

These strange flying objects were coined the "ghost rockets," and unlike back in the early 1930s when media coverage of the ghost fliers was somewhat muted and provincial, news of the ghost rockets went around the world in a flash.

They were *so* puzzling, in fact, that for the first time, high-level military officials went on record as saying the mysterious flying objects might not be of this earth.

The first sightings were reported in Swedish newspapers in February 1946. As with the ghost fliers thirteen years before, once word was out, sighting reports began to cascade. People reported seeing the strange projectiles all over Sweden that spring and into the summer.

The peak came between August 9 and 11, 1946. Coincidentally, this is the height of the annual Perseid meteor showers, and there's no doubt that within that time frame a large number of the sightings *were*, in fact, meteors.

But not all of them.

Almost from the beginning, there were differing descriptions of the ghost rockets. Early examples were depicted as fireballs or unknown light phenomena, not unlike some foo fighters. But two images eventually became predominant: a fast-moving missile-shaped object 12 to 15 feet long with wings, and a similarly sized object without wings. Sometimes a hissing or humming sound was heard coming from them, but mostly these mystery missiles were silent.

Most intriguing, though, was that not only did many people see the ghost rockets flying horizontally—belying the meteor theory—and doing maneuvers, including pulling 180-degree turns, but some witnesses actually saw two or more flying in formation!

The ghost rockets displayed another bizarre trait: a tendency to crash into lakes. The topography of upper Scandinavia is pockmarked with lakes, many of which are long and deep, and in the summer, mostly free of ice. But the landscape is also thick with tall mountains, yawning valleys and thousands of square miles of empty tundra. Yet dozens of witnesses saw ghost rockets falling into lakes, almost as if directed there.

One famous case happened on July 19, 1946. Witnesses saw a rocket-shaped object fall into Lake Kölmjärv, in far northeast Sweden. The military quickly cordoned off the area and did an extensive search of the lake's bottom. Yet nothing was ever found.

The Swedish government became so concerned about the ghost rockets that they violated their country's famous neutrality and secretly implored Great Britain to send them some modern radar systems. Once these were in place, the Swedish military began searching for the mysterious flying objects electronically. The result: An astounding 200 of the ghost rockets were eventually tracked on radar.

The Swedish reached out for help a second time during the crisis, this time to the United States. On August 20, 1946, two prominent Americans arrived in Stockholm. One was General David Sarnoff, the man who went on to found RCA and the NBC network. Ostensibly Sarnoff was in Sweden to study the market for broadcast equipment. But Sarnoff, a member of Dwight Eisenhower's war staff, was actually there to be briefed on the ghost rockets by the Swedish military.

The second man was none other than Jimmy Doolittle, the hero of the famous "Thirty Seconds Over Tokyo" raid. Doolittle was a VP of the Shell oil company at the time, and his cover story was that he was supposedly inspecting Shell facilities in Sweden. But like Sarnoff, he, too, was there to investigate the ghost rocket situation firsthand.

Both men met with officers high in the Swedish military and were briefed on the mysterious objects, specifically those cases that had been picked up on radar. On returning to the United States, Doolittle and Sarnoff reported their findings to the Central Intelligence Group (CIG), a precursor to the CIA. Shortly afterward, the CIG delivered a top secret report to President Truman on the subject. And at first, this report seemed to have solved the mystery.

In fact, it pointed to a likely launching point for the ghost rockets.

A place called Peenemünde.

Located on Germany's Baltic coast, Peenemünde was the world's first rocket base, the place where the Nazis developed and flew their V-1 and V-2 rocket-powered wonder weapons.

The theory conjured up by U.S. and Swedish intelligence services was that the ghost rockets were actually Russian updates of captured V-1 and V-2 rockets and that the Soviets were using the former German base to launch them.

The Swedes were so sure this was the case, they installed a press embargo on the nation's newspapers, ordering them not to print the locations of ghost rocket crash sites, believing this would give the Russians valuable information on how far their new missiles were traveling.

The theory sounded good, especially in light of rising tensions between the West and their soon-to-be former ally, the Soviet Union.

But it was all wrong.

* * *

True, Peenemünde had been overrun by the Russian army near the end of World War II, and by 1946, it was part of Soviet-controlled East Germany.

But the advancing Soviet troops had found most of the rocket facility in ruins, the result of both intensive Allied bombing and the retreating Germans not wanting to leave anything of value behind. Rebuilding the base would have been a huge undertaking for the Russians and something they would have had to do in complete secrecy.

Moreover, even in the best of times, the Germans could barely launch fifteen V-1 buzz bombs in a day. There were more than two hundred ghost rocket sightings reported on July 9 alone. And on August 11, more than three hundred of the strange objects were seen just around Stockholm.

Launching this many V-1-type rockets on a daily basis would require a huge facility, equipped with launch pads, fuel storage and transport, command and control buildings and hundreds if not thousands of support personnel, all in a day when rocket technology was still in its infancy.

If not at Peenemünde, then where were these missile-launching bases? Who was manning them? Where were they getting their supplies, their core materials? Their fuel?

And what would be the reason to launch hundreds of missiles that all seemed to land in lakes and then, quite literally, disappear? Why would the war-ravaged Russians publicly fire hundreds of rockets into a neighboring neutral country?

Finally, how would a Russian secret missile program up near the Baltics account for further ghost rocket sightings reported over Greece, France and even the United States?

It was only later that the West's intelligence services confirmed that there was no renewed activity at Peenemünde. Whatever remained of the German rocket base had been moved to Poland by the Russians.

In other words, the official explanation of what the ghost rockets were was not an explanation at all.

Ghost rocket sightings lasted throughout 1946. In all, about two thousand were sighted from May to December that year. Then just like the ghost fliers, the ghost rockets eventually faded away.

So *what* were they?

Sherlock Holmes is famous for saying: "When you have eliminated the impossible, whatever remains, however improbable, must be the truth."

Thus the Swedes were forced to look at other explanations.

As recorded in Jerome Clark's *The UFO Encyclopedia (Second Edition): The Phenomenon from the Beginning* on October 10, the Swedish Defence Staff released this statement on the subject: "Most observations are vague and must be treated very skeptically. In some cases, however, clear, unambiguous observations have been made that cannot be explained as natural phenomena, Swedish aircraft, or imagination on the part of the observer."

Apparently the U.S. military didn't disagree. A top secret U.S. Air Force document from November 1948 hinted that some military investigators believed the ghost rockets had extraterrestrial origins.

Declassified nearly five decades later, the document states:

"When [our] officers recently visited the Swedish Air Intelligence Service, the question [of the ghost rockets' origin] was put to the Swedes. Their answer was that some reliable and fully technically qualified people had reached the conclusion that these phenomena are obviously the result of a high technical skill which cannot be credited to any presently known culture on Earth. They are therefore assuming that these objects originate from some previously unknown or unidentified technology, possibly outside the Earth."

As unlikely as it might seem, Laurance S. Rockefeller, of the American billionaire Rockefellers, had a serious interest in the UFO question. Through his auspices in 1995, a sober, well-documented paper called "The Best Available Evidence" was produced (see: UFOScience.org).

The report contains this story: On the morning of August 14, 1946, a Swedish air force pilot was flying over central Sweden when he saw an object soaring along slightly above him and about a mile away. It was one of the ghost rockets. He estimated it was traveling about 400 miles per hour.

The pilot reported that not only was the object maintaining a stable horizontal altitude over the ground, it was basically following the terrain, meaning, if a mountain loomed up before it, it simply climbed enough to get over the mountain before returning to its previous altitude. But terrain-following technology is something that wasn't even attempted until the 1960s and not really perfected until the 1980s.

Eric Malmberg was secretary of Sweden's Defence Staff committee during the time of the ghost rockets. He was interviewed on the topic forty years later by UFO researchers

Anders Liljegren and Clas Svahn. Contained in their paper "Ghost Rockets and Phantom Aircraft" from the anthology *Phenomenon—Forty Years of Flying Saucers,* Malmberg told them something both perplexing and chilling.

Talking about what was seen over Sweden that strange summer, he said: "If the observations were correct, many details suggest that it was some kind of a cruise missile. But nobody had that kind of sophisticated technology in 1946."

11

America vs. the Flying Saucers

The "Era of Flying Saucers" began on June 24, 1947.

That day, Idaho businessman Kenneth Arnold was flying his private plane over the Cascade Mountains in Washington State when he spotted nine brightly shining objects streaking across the afternoon sky.

In Arnold's own words, the conditions were clear that day and the air was calm. He was on course to Yakima, Washington, as part of a business trip, when suddenly he was startled by a flash of light to his left. At first Arnold thought he'd strayed into the path of another airplane. But on seeing that the sky immediately around him was empty, his eyes were drawn to Mount Rainier about 20 miles off his left wing. There he saw the line of shiny objects flying at about 9,500 feet, heading south. It was these objects reflecting the sun that had attracted Arnold attention in the first place.

As recounted in Jerome Clark's *The UFO Encyclopedia,*

Arnold said that he was unable to make out their shapes for the first few seconds. But once they passed Mount Rainier, he saw their outlines against the snow and realized they were flat and tailless. Like a "half a pie plate," was his initial description.

Arnold's sighting was no quick event. He had the flying objects in view for more than two and a half minutes. In that time, he saw the strange craft perform some incredible maneuvers, such as all turning as one as they wound their way between the mountaintops.

The objects were also moving very fast. As Arnold watched them fly between Mount Rainier and Mount Adams, he calculated the objects had traveled almost 50 miles in a minute and forty-five seconds. That works out to 1,700 miles per hour, nearly three times the speed of sound, faster by far than any known airplane of the day.

All this led Arnold to assume the objects were some kind of secret military aircraft.

Only after he left Yakima and flew on to Pendleton, Oregon, and spoke to some fellow pilots did Arnold begin to think what he'd seen might *not* belong to the U.S. military—or anyone else's.

No tails, flying near Mach 3, being able to maneuver themselves between mountaintops with ease? At the time, nothing on earth could fly that way. Nothing man-made, anyway.

Word of Arnold's sighting spread quickly, and by the next day, he was telling his story to a local Washington newspaper. And although he had indeed previously described the objects as looking like half a pie plate, Arnold was later quoted as saying they moved like saucers skipping across the water. Thus, the term "flying saucer" was born.

No sooner had the story hit the newswires, though, than something strange happened: Suddenly people all over the United States began seeing flying saucers.

Just on June 28 alone, an army pilot flying an F-51 Mustang near Lake Mead, Nevada, spotted five circular objects go by his fighter's right wing; two farmers in Wisconsin saw ten saucer-shaped objects fly over them at high speed; and four army officers at Maxwell airfield in Montgomery, Alabama, watched an unusual circular object perform inconceivable midair maneuvers for more than twenty minutes.

The next day, June 29, a bus driver in Des Moines saw four circular objects flash through the sky at high speed; in Jacksonville, Oregon, a chevron formation of saucers was seen by people leaving a church; and in New Mexico, a car full of rocket scientists traveling near the White Sands Proving Ground spotted a silvery disk traveling at an astonishing velocity.

On and on it went . . . On June 30, an F-80 jet pilot reported seeing two gray circular objects while in flight. On July 3, an astronomer in Maine spotted ten saucers flying in perfect formation, and a family of ten in Idaho saw eight huge circular objects actually *land*. On July 4, a coastguardsman near Seattle, Washington, took a photo of a circular flying object; more saucers were spotted over Portland, Oregon; Milwaukee, Wisconsin; Vancouver, Washington; and Emmett, Idaho. In fact, more than twenty other people in Washington State had seen the same mystery disks Arnold had reported back on June 24.

Many unexplained things had been spotted flying through earth's skies for most of the century: the scareships of 1909, the ghost fliers of 1933–34, the foo fighters of World War II, the ghost rockets of 1946. But for whatever reason, Arnold's sighting was the one that grabbed the headlines, the one that made the splash. And because no one in the media or the U.S. military ever thought to link Arnold's saucers to these other mysterious events, Arnold's aerial enigmas were presented as something new—and, in a way, something uniquely American. Finally, these strange flying things had a name that everyone could understand.

Kenneth Arnold's story is well-known and has been heavily researched with more details than can be properly presented here. Some highly respected ufologists have pointed out that while the U.S. Air Force eventually concluded what Arnold saw was a "mirage," no official investigation has ever been conducted on the famous sighting, and no definitive explanation has ever been given for what happened that day.

But an even stranger, if lesser-known, flying saucer story cropped up around the same time as the Arnold encounter. Among other things, this episode featured what might have been the U.S. military's first serious attempt to actually study a UFO sighting.

It also revealed a dark side to the brand-new science of investigating unidentified flying objects.

It's known as the Maury Island Incident.

A somewhat murky affair, many different versions have been told over the years, fascinating some UFO researchers while causing extreme *agita* in others. Controversial or not, the following account contains those elements most people agree on.

It is said to have started on the afternoon of June 21, three days *before* the famous Kenneth Arnold sighting. A man named Harold Dahl was piloting a workboat in Puget Sound, near the port of Tacoma, Washington. With him were his son, two crewmen and the family dog. They were out on the sound looking for stray logs. Tacoma is close to logging country, and Dahl worked for a company that rounded up any loose cut trees that might have wound up in the harbor.

Dahl was sailing near Maury Island, a piece of land about three miles north of Tacoma. It was a cloudy day, and the waters of the sound were choppy. Suddenly the boat's passengers became aware of six strange objects hovering about 2,000 feet above them. At first Dahl and his passengers thought they were balloons, but that idea quickly passed. The objects were about 100 feet long and shaped like doughnuts, complete with holes in the middle. They looked to be built of shiny metal with portholes around their outer rims and one continuous window lining the inside of the center opening. They made no noise.

Almost immediately, Dahl and crew saw one of the objects begin to falter. It dropped far below the others before pulling up directly above Dahl's workboat. Fearing this object might crash into them, Dahl hastily headed for nearby Maury Island.

The boat's occupants scrambled onto land, and from there they watched as the other five objects closed in on the wavering saucer and started circling it. Grabbing his camera, Dahl snapped off a handful of photos.

After a few minutes of circling, one of the five objects drew even closer to the ailing disk, making physical contact with it. This maneuver seemed to give the distressed object a boost of energy, as if being jumped by a battery. Suddenly the object began expelling material from the hole in its center. First, there was a rain of thin metal strips that looked like scraps of newspaper. But then came a deluge of what Dahl described as a metallic slaglike material—twenty *tons* of it.

This storm of weird metal came crashing down all around Dahl and company, damaging their boat, injuring Dahl's son and killing the family dog. Dahl frantically tried calling for help—but his radio had mysteriously stopped working.

The boat's occupants scrambled for cover and stayed there until the downpour of slag stopped. At this point, the troubled UFO seemed to recover its faculties. It rejoined the other five objects, and together, the formation climbed to a tremendous height and quickly disappeared.

Shaken by what he'd seen, Dahl hastily recovered some of the mysterious metal and then rushed back to Tacoma where his son was treated for his injury.

By his own account, Dahl told no one about the events on Maury Island.

The next morning, June 22, a stranger appeared at Dahl's door.

Dahl described him as a male in his early forties, dressed in a black suit and driving a black car. At first, Dahl thought he was an insurance salesman. But after the man invited him to breakfast, Dahl suspected the visitor was from the government or the military. In any case, Dahl accepted the invitation.

Once at breakfast, the stranger asked Dahl some unusual

questions, such as: "Are you happy with your job?" and "Are you happy with your family?"

Then, more chilling, the man proceeded to tell Dahl many intimate details of his UFO sighting on Maury Island the day before. Dahl was shocked; the man knew information Dahl hadn't told anybody since returning from the incident.

The stranger then advised Dahl to forget what occurred and insinuated that if Dahl spoke any further about what he'd seen, it wouldn't be good for him or his family.

With that, the man left.

The implied threat from this individual, possibly the first American "Man in Black" episode on record, did not stop Dahl, though. He reported to work later that day and told everything to his boss, a man named Fred Crisman.

By some accounts, Crisman, a World War II fighter pilot, didn't believe Dahl's story. This was no surprise, as the world was not yet aware of the term "flying saucer," or UFO, for that matter. So Crisman went to Maury Island to see for himself, only to observe a strange flying object there, too. He also recovered some of the mysterious slaglike metal.

A short time later, Crisman sent a sample of the material to a man in Chicago named Ray Palmer. Palmer was editor of the magazine *Amazing Science Fiction*. Intrigued by the material and the tale that went with it, Palmer asked a rookie reporter to go to Tacoma and write a story about the Maury Island event.

That novice reporter was none other than Kenneth Arnold.

* * *

Arnold flew to Tacoma on July 29, a little more than a month after the Maury Island Incident.

On arrival, he called to reserve a room at the well-regarded Winthrop Hotel. But, some reports say, Arnold was told a room had already been set aside for him, though the hotel staff had no idea who'd made the reservation. That was just a hint of the weirdness to come.

Arnold got in touch with Dahl, but at first his subject was reluctant to meet. Reports say that Dahl had had an unusual streak of bad luck in the five weeks following his UFO encounter. He'd nearly been fired, his son had gone missing and his wife was ill. Whether it was these episodes or the meeting with the man in the black suit that had shaken him, at first, Arnold was met by a brick wall.

Dahl eventually agreed to talk to Arnold; by some reports, they met the next day, July 30, at the Winthrop. Dahl gave Arnold some of the material he said he'd found on Maury Island, though to Arnold it looked like ordinary slag, something that would come from an iron smelter.

But then Dahl's boss, Fred Crisman, joined the meeting. He told Arnold that there were indeed *tons* of the slag-like material on Maury Island, a place nowhere near an iron smelter.

Sometime around this point, reports say Arnold reached out for expert help. After his own sighting, Arnold had befriended a commercial airline pilot named E. J. Smith. Smith had spotted a set of shiny disks skipping through the sky near Boise, Idaho, just a few days after Arnold's famous sighting, in an encounter almost identical to Arnold's.

Smith in turn recommended that Arnold get military

intelligence involved. After his own sighting, Smith had been questioned by an Army Air Corps officer named Lieutenant Frank Brown; Smith now contacted Brown and told him what had happened at Maury Island.

Besieged by reports of flying saucers from all over America, the U.S. military was getting concerned that the mysterious aerial objects might actually be Russian secret weapons. So army intelligence jumped at the chance to recover something that had fallen out of the Maury Island object.

Accompanied by another intelligence officer named Captain William Davidson, Lieutenant Brown took off in a B-25 bomber from Hamilton airfield in California and flew to McChord airfield just outside Tacoma. The military officers joined the others in Arnold's room at the Winthrop Hotel on the afternoon of July 31.

According to Arnold, who later wrote about the meeting in a book, Dahl repeated his story for the military officers. They also discussed the photos Dahl had taken on the day of the incident, which had come out distorted and useless, as if they'd been exposed to X-rays.

But then things took another weird turn. While the meeting was going on, a reporter from the *Tacoma Times* called Arnold and repeated back to him practically everything Dahl and Crisman were saying to the military officers. The reporter said he got the information from an anonymous phone caller, even though no one beyond Arnold's hotel room was privy to what was being said. Completely bewildered by this bizarre turn of events, Arnold searched the room for listening devices but found none.

Still, the anonymous caller continued feeding intimate information on the meeting to the newspaperman, baffling both the reporter and the people gathered in Arnold's room.

It seemed that someone unseen was able to peer in on them and hear exactly what was being said.

By most accounts, after Brown and Davidson listened to the Maury Island story, the military officers hastily took their leave. One report said Brown and Davidson told the others they had to return to the Hamilton air base that night because the following day was the first ever Air Force Day. Whatever the reason, the pair left, taking a box of the mysterious slaglike material with them.

Returning to nearby McChord air base where their B-25 was waiting, Brown and Davidson had a quick briefing with the base intelligence officer. Then they boarded their airplane and took off, carrying a box of classified material with them.

A short time later, both men were dead.

The B-25 Brown and Davidson were flying crashed near the Washington-Oregon border, not far from Mount Rainier, where Kenneth Arnold had spotted the first flying saucers just a month earlier.

Local newspaper reports hinted broadly that the plane had been sabotaged, and the story would become even more intriguing when a spokesman for McChord air base at first denied but then confirmed that the two officers were indeed carrying classified information when their plane went down.

It was Crisman who told Arnold about the B-25's crash. The next day, Crisman and Dahl met with Arnold once again at the hotel to discuss the tragic event. At some point soon afterward, Arnold decided he'd had enough. He contacted Ray Palmer, the magazine editor, and told him he couldn't gather enough material to do a proper story. Then Arnold prepared to leave Tacoma.

What was the real reason Arnold wanted out? Some reports say the same Tacoma reporter who'd informed him of the leaks coming from his room told Arnold he was involved in something that was beyond his power, suggesting he get out of town until things blew over.

There were also reports that Brown and Davidson had passed on the same recommendation to Arnold shortly before they died.

In any case, Arnold decided to take the advice. But upon takeoff from Tacoma, Arnold's plane suffered a mysterious malfunction. A critical fuel valve in his engine had either gotten turned off or had inexplicably frozen over. Either way, Arnold suddenly found himself on the verge of crashing.

It was only because Arnold was a seasoned pilot that he was able to land his plane safely. Yet, had he been airborne just a little longer, or flying just a little higher, there's no doubt he would have been killed in the resulting crash.

Some UFO historians contend Dahl and Crisman later admitted to the FBI that the Maury Island Incident was all a hoax. There had been no UFOs. No mysterious alien substance. They had only been telling magazine editor Ray Palmer what he wanted to hear.

But on closer examination, exactly what kind of hoax would this be? How could anybody come up with a plan to fool the government, the military and a national magazine with a story about flying saucers, when "flying saucers" did not come into the national vernacular until three days *after* the supposed event? And how could there be twenty tons of the "slaglike material" on Maury Island beach when there is no smelter anywhere near the lonely spit of land? And who was the mysterious man in black?

Fred Crisman later told *Fate* magazine that any report that he called the Maury Island Incident a hoax was a "bald-faced lie." Kenneth Arnold as well believed something happened in Puget Sound that day, talking about the incident at length many years later at the First International UFO Congress in Chicago.

And reportedly, no less than J. Edgar Hoover, head of the FBI at the time, believed the incident was not a deception. Many of the Maury Island accounts cite a message sent on August 14, 1947, in which Hoover was quoted as saying: "It would appear that Dahl and Crisman did not admit the hoax to the army officers . . ." To which his special agent in charge of the FBI's Seattle office responded: "Please be advised that Dahl did not admit to Brown that his story was a hoax but only stated that if questioned by authorities he was going to *say* it was a hoax because he did not want any further trouble."

Fred Crisman died in 1975. Harold Dahl died in 1982, and Arnold, in 1984.

But many questions still surround the strange Maury Island Incident.

The slaglike material was eventually tested. Some reports say it was ordinary slag; others claim it didn't contain enough iron to qualify as such.

Some accounts claim the FBI reported that Dahl's son disappeared in the middle of all the controversy, showing up in Montana, supposedly with no recollection of how he got there. Still another report says Dahl's wife later stabbed him because he wouldn't tell the FBI exactly what happened that day off Maury Island. And supposedly, the newspaper reporter involved in the mysterious tipster episode died two weeks after the incident.

According to some who have studied the case closely (such as noted UFO researcher Jenny Randles) and who know the ins and outs of how intelligence agencies work, the overload of information, disinformation, rumors and half-truths that haunt the Maury Island case seem to bear the earmarks of a sophisticated intelligence operation, possibly one put in place to discredit Arnold's original UFO sighting.

But perhaps the strangest aspect of all of this involved Fred Crisman.

In 1968, he was called before a congressional committee to testify about his whereabouts on November 22, 1963—the day President John F. Kennedy was assassinated in Dallas, Texas.

12

What Happened at Roswell?

Probably the most publicized flying saucer incident in history is known as the "Roswell Crash." Even people with only a passing interest in the UFO phenomenon know at least a little bit about it.

On or around July 4, 1947—just days after Kenneth Arnold's famous sighting, and while the United States was caught in the throes of saucer mania—a spacecraft reportedly crashed on a ranch in a remote part of New Mexico. A local ranch hand spotted the impact site and recovered bits of wreckage that looked a lot like aluminum foil and pieces of balsa wood. These items were scattered over a wide area.

The ranch hand took some of the fragments to Roswell, New Mexico, which was actually about 30 miles away from the debris field. He contacted local authorities, and soon enough, the military was involved.

Close to the town of Roswell was Roswell Army Air

Field. At that time, the Roswell base was the only military facility in the United States whose aircraft were equipped to carry atomic weapons. This only added to the crash mystery.

The air force eventually took ownership of the ranch hand's fragments as well as all the debris found on the ranch itself, though a few civilians managed to view several of the pieces beforehand.

After looking over these remains and hearing the ranch hand's story as well as stories of other residents who'd seen a strange object flying over the area during the night in question, the air force made a startling announcement: They said they'd captured a flying saucer.

This declaration, issued in the form of a press release by Roswell's base commander, was accompanied by a photo showing some of the "saucer's" pieces.

The story made the local headlines, and soon enough the events at Roswell were news across the country. Again, it helps to remember that at the time, the summer of 1947, people from every state in the union were reporting flying saucers. Now it seemed as if the great flying saucer mystery was about to be solved.

But the excitement only lasted one day. Twenty-four hours after making the startling announcement, the air force reversed itself and said the debris found—the aluminum strips and the balsa wood—were actually parts of a weather balloon that had crashed on the remote ranch.

And for the most part, the public believed the air force. The story went away—for more than thirty years.

It was revived in 1978 when a UFO researcher interviewed a military officer who was part of the original air force team that retrieved the Roswell wreckage. For the first time this officer said he believed the debris wasn't a balloon, but rather *was* part of a wrecked alien spacecraft and that the military had covered up the crash.

This interview led to an article in the *National Enquirer*. Then came books touting an almost completely different version of the previously accepted events. By the early 1980s, the speed and range of the media had increased a hundredfold from 1947. The "new" story of Roswell suddenly took off.

This time around it was claimed that the debris found on the desolate ranch had possessed incredible properties. The aluminumlike foil now had superstrength and the ability to "unfold itself." The balsa sticks now had indecipherable hieroglyphics written on them. And people were coming forward to say they'd seen alien bodies taken from the crash site as well.

Most damning was the claim that the air force's retraction back in July 1947 wasn't a retraction at all. It was the beginning of a massive cover-up.

The tale quickly grew to immense proportions, including reports of a top secret U.S. military mission to retrieve more crashed saucers and more dead and dying aliens, at the same time terrifying the local citizenry and threatening witnesses with bodily harm if they didn't remain silent. Suddenly there were claims of almost a *dozen* UFO crash sites in the Roswell area, with alien bodies strewn about everywhere.

Finally, two UFO authors, Kal Korff and Karl T. Pflock, brought most people back down to earth. Korff's *The Ros-*

well UFO Crash: What They Don't Want You To Know and Pflock's *Roswell: Inconvenient Facts and the Will to Believe* pretty much sought to blow the lid off the Roswell "crash."

Korff, for instance, went after the so-called witnesses involved with one of the most extreme books perpetuating the Roswell myth. Though ninety people were supposedly interviewed for this book, only twenty-five names actually appeared in it, of which only seven actually saw the "crash debris" and only five had actually handled this debris.

Pflock did some similar digging, revealing that of the three-hundred-plus people supposedly interviewed for another disputed Roswell book, only forty-one could be considered credible, only twenty-three of them might have actually seen the debris and of them only seven mentioned the fragments might be of an extraterrestrial origin.

Both authors also pointed out that anyone who'd come forward claiming to have seen alien bodies either had credibility problems or had changed their stories frequently.

The U.S. Air Force released two reports in the 1990s dealing with the controversy. In them they revealed the debris was not from a crashed alien spacecraft but rather from a top secret intelligence-gathering balloon, as well as its "kite," which was the nickname for a radar reflector that helped track the balloon on its flight.

The balloon's purpose, as revealed by the air force, was to drift close to the Soviet Union and pick up sound vibrations that might indicate the Russians were testing a nuclear weapon.

The U.S. military was loath to give out this information back in 1947, so to a certain extent there *was* a cover-up.

But it might not have been the cover-up everyone thought it was. In this case, at least, it seems the air force could be believed.

Books still come out promoting the more fantastic Roswell line. The town itself is a huge tourist attraction, complete with a UFO museum. Roswell has been featured in movies, TV shows, comic books, sci-fi novels and even toys.

But after all is said and done, if the question is: What happened at Roswell—or more specifically, did some kind of *extraterrestrial* event happen at Roswell? Then the answer is: Probably not.

13

Opportunity Lost

In the wake of the Arnold sighting and the tidal wave of flying saucer reports that followed, by midsummer of 1947, the fledgling U.S. Air Force found itself forced to investigate the UFO phenomenon.

The bulk of this scrutiny fell to the Air Technical Intelligence Center (ATIC). It was the part of the air force charged with studying problems facing America's national security, such as new weapons being developed by potential enemies. By all reports, the personnel at the ATIC were high-quality, clearheaded scientists and engineers, all well respected within the military community.

So when in September 1947 they generated their preliminary internal report on the flying saucer matter, the air force took it seriously. And as it turned out, the ATIC investigators came up with a startling conclusion: They believed flying saucers were real. As recounted in the renowned *Report on Unidentified Flying Objects*, their exact words were:

"The phenomenon is not visionary or fictitious." The ATIC urged the mystery be studied further.

The air force followed their advice. In January 1948, Project Sign was established at Wright-Patterson Air Force Base in Ohio. Its mission was to evaluate all information concerning flying saucer sightings that might pose a risk to U.S. national security. To emphasize the gravity of the matter, anything Project Sign produced was to be classified as "Secret."

If there was ever a moment the U.S. military thought flying saucers should be studied objectively, this was it.

Meanwhile, the ATIC had no shortage of incidents to investigate. Reports of flying saucer sightings continued to pour in.

Hundreds were seen across the United States in 1948. But three incidents were particularly noteworthy, with one being particularly tragic.

On the afternoon of January 7, 1948, Kentucky State Police received reports of a large circular object flying over the city of Maysville. This same object was also spotted by control tower personnel at Godman Air Force Base, which is located near Fort Knox.

Captain Thomas Mantell, a pilot in the Kentucky Air National Guard, was leading a flight of four F-51 Mustangs that happened to be passing through the area at the time of the sighting. Godman's control tower asked the fighter pilots to check out the strange object. Low fuel forced one of the Mustangs to drop out, but Mantell and the two other remaining F-51s climbed to investigate.

Again, as quoted in the *Report on Unidentified Flying*

Objects, when Mantell reached 15,000 feet, he told Godman tower: "The object is directly above me now. It appears to be a metallic object . . . and it is of tremendous size . . . I'm still climbing . . . I'm trying to close in for a better look."

Mustangs are propeller-driven craft not generally equipped with the oxygen gear pilots need for flying at high altitudes. Passing up through 22,000 feet, and close to surpassing their safe altitude limit, the two other pilots turned back.

But Mantell kept climbing . . .

A couple of hours later, Mantell's plane was found on a farm near Franklin, Kentucky, crumpled and burning. The pilot was still strapped inside, headless. His watch had stopped at 3:18 P.M., the moment his plane hit the ground.

Why an experienced pilot like Mantell would so foolishly climb above a safe altitude remains a mystery. His last words leave no doubt, though, that he was mesmerized by whatever he was chasing.

His death was highly publicized, generating rumors that he'd been *shot down* by a UFO. This in turn fostered the idea that maybe the earth's mysterious visitors weren't so friendly.

Six months later, on the night of July 24, 1948, an Eastern Airlines DC-3 was en route from Houston to Atlanta with Captain Clarence Chiles and copilot John Whitted at the controls. Flying over the city of Montgomery, Alabama, a dull red glowing object suddenly appeared in front of them. Both pilots described the object as being about the size of a B-29 bomber, but with no wings or tail.

The pilots were shocked when the object headed right at them. Before they could react, it streaked by their starboard side, barely missing a midair collision. As it went by, the pilots saw that the wingless craft had a row of windows running down its side. The UFO then climbed quickly and disappeared.

As it turned out, people at Robbins Air Force Base, located near Macon, Georgia, also saw an unknown object about thirty minutes before the DC-3's encounter. The witnesses' description matched that of Chiles and Whitted. It was later determined no other planes were in the area of the sighting.

The third perplexing UFO incident of 1948 happened a few months later. Lieutenant George Gorman of the North Dakota Air National Guard was piloting an F-51, the same kind of aircraft as the late Captain Mantell, on a routine night-training mission. Gorman was approaching his airfield when the control tower asked him to check out an unidentified object that had been detected flying in the vicinity of the base.

Gorman did as asked and soon found himself within 1,000 feet of a brightly-lit disk-shaped object. But as he tried to get closer, the UFO started heading for him. Diving out of the way to avoid a collision, Gorman turned, only to see that the UFO had turned as well and was once again heading right for him. Gorman did not veer off until the last moment, but then found himself climbing with the object, straight up to 14,000 feet. That's when Gorman's F-51 began to falter. But as he leveled out, the UFO leveled out about a half mile above him. They each made a series of tight maneuvers, but suddenly the UFO came right at him for a *third* time. This time, though, the UFO broke off, went straight up and disappeared into the night at high speed.

Gorman finally gave up the chase and landed.

In UFO lore, this incident is commonly referred to as "the dogfight with a flying saucer."

But just like the previous two stories, it has never been explained.

In September 1948, the ATIC prepared a second, lengthier study on flying saucers. It was sent to General Hoyt Vandenberg, then air force chief of staff.

Following up on its preliminary report, which had stated that flying saucers did "exist," the ATIC investigators had now studied whether the saucers were something man-made—by the Soviet Union, or even perhaps by the U.S. military itself. However, they concluded this was not the case.

Which left only one other explanation: Those flying saucer episodes that could not be explained must have some kind of extraterrestrial origin.

This had to be an exciting time for the ATIC researchers as, by their own words, they, specifically, and the world as a whole, were on the verge of investigating something whose implications for the human race were enormous.

Unfortunately, the air force didn't see it that way.

While officially General Vandenberg returned the report to ATIC under the pretext of wanting more "proof," unofficially, as pointed out by many UFO researchers, Vandenberg was essentially letting the ATIC know that they'd told him something he didn't want to hear. Either the U.S. military didn't want to admit that it didn't understand UFOs and therefore couldn't protect the country against them, or they knew what they were but had decided to keep the news from the public—that was the big question. But there was one thing they weren't going to do: They would not go on record as saying flying saucers were from outer space.

This was the moment when the door that was opened with Project Sign suddenly began to close again. Looking back on it, a total of six months of study had been done on what might have been one of the most momentous discoveries of all time.

More time went by, during which flying saucer reports continued almost unabated. In December 1949, the U.S. Air Force's UFO project, now known as "Project Grudge," released yet another report.

Despite what would seem to be mountains of evidence to the contrary, the report stated that no conclusive evidence had been found that could prove or disprove the existence of these unidentified flying objects.

This is what the air force wanted to hear.

The report went on to say, in effect, that all UFO sightings fell into two categories: one being instances that could be explained away, such as mistaken astronomical phenomena or aircraft or balloons, and the other, hoaxes, hallucinations, delusions or reports made by crackpots.

Or as reported in Major Donald Keyhoe's *Flying Saucers from Outer Space*, one air force colonel famously put it: "Behind nearly every UFO report stands a crackpot, a religious crank, a publicity hound or a malicious joke."

And with that, the U.S. Air Force shut down the project, eager to get out of the business of investigating flying saucers. It is there that many researchers believe the U.S. military's cover-up of UFOs began—something many claim remains in place today.

Whatever the case, the door seemed closed for good.

But then, six months later, in June 1950, communist North Korea invaded South Korea, igniting the world's first major post–World War II conflict.

And that would change everything.

PART FIVE

The 1950s

14

Saucers Over Korea

In September 1950, two months after the beginning of the Korean conflict, a trio of U.S. Navy fighter-bombers launched from an aircraft carrier cruising off the coast of the war-torn country. One after the other, they climbed to 10,000 feet and headed for the skies over the communist north. Beneath their wings were several tons of bombs.

The fighting in Korea over the previous two months had been brutal. During some particularly dark days in July and August, the U.S. military, woefully downsized after World War II, found itself and its UN allies nearly pushed off the Korean Peninsula altogether.

The strategic situation changed when General Douglas MacArthur led a surprise seaborne attack on the communist-held port of Inchon, cutting the enemy forces in two. MacArthur's dramatic action eventually led to the communists being forced out of South Korea entirely and then pursued into the north. By late September 1950, the United States was finally on the offensive.

The mission for the three carrier-launched navy attack planes this early morning was to bomb a North Korean truck convoy that had been spotted moving through a valley about 100 miles south of the Chinese border.

The sun was just coming up when the navy planes reached their target. Each aircraft carried two crewmembers—a pilot and a radar operator/gunner, also known as the RO. Each plane was also carrying about 4,000 pounds of munitions.

As they were preparing for their bombing runs, the planes' radar operators, intent on getting a fix on the targeted convoy, instead found themselves staring at a pair of huge shadows crossing the valley floor two miles below. Looking out in front of them, the navy fliers were astonished to see a pair of saucer-shaped objects approaching from the northwest— *they* were causing the giant shadows. Incredibly, these objects were traveling close to Mach 2, or 1,200 miles per hour, twice as fast as any military aircraft of the day.

Most astonishing, though, was their size. The navy crews estimated the silver-colored objects were nearly 700 feet in diameter—more than two football fields put together!

What were these things? Certainly neither of the war's combatants had any aircraft the size of two football fields, or the ability to travel at such blisteringly high speeds. The largest combat plane flying the skies during the Korean War was the U.S. Air Force's B-29 bomber, a plane easily recognized by pilots on both sides. These were definitely *not* B-29s.

One of the navy ROs instinctively went to arm his guns. But at that moment, his radar set malfunctioned. The

RO ran a quick checklist of adjustments, hoping to get the radar back, but nothing worked. His equipment was being jammed.

The RO next tried calling the carrier, but his radio wasn't working, either. He switched frequencies, only to hear a strange buzzing at every turn. His radio was being jammed, too.

At this point the gigantic flying objects were about a mile in front of the navy attack planes. Suddenly, the saucers stopped in midair, changed direction and swung around toward the three navy planes. In seconds the saucers were effortlessly maneuvering both above and below the fighter-bombers, circling them, as if inspecting them.

Then just as abruptly, the saucers spun around again, turned back toward the northwest and left the area at high speed.

Warfare had changed substantially in the five years since the end of World War II. By the time the Korean Conflict began, military technology in particular had taken a great leap forward, especially in the area of combat aircraft and air operations.

Suddenly there were hundreds of high-speed jet air-planes flying through the crowded airspace above the Korean Peninsula, an area less than one-third the size of Texas. At the same time, there had been a proliferation of radar devices. These were not just ground-based or shipborne; powerful radar sets were also being carried inside all those high-speed aircraft.

This meant any strange flying thing could now be seen

not just by human observers, but by many, *many* electronic eyes as well.

Yet at the same time, the U.S. military, and principally the U.S. Air Force, was shackled to its new policy of labeling all "unexplainable" flying saucer reports as being the result of "crackpots, hoaxes or delusions." This was hard to do when, in addition to the sudden increase in all this warmaking technology, the U.S. had hundreds of highly qualified and, in many cases, combat-hardened pilots airborne at any given time. When these pilots began reporting UFOs flying over Korea, the military found itself in an uncomfortable position: If they were to follow the new policy, they'd have to label any pilot who saw a UFO either a crackpot, a hoaxer or delusional.

To avoid this predicament, anything strange seen in the sky *had* to be explained away so as not to disparage the men the U.S. was counting on to help win the war.

The results were sometimes darkly humorous.

On January 29, 1952, two B-29 bombers flying in the area of Wonsan, North Korea, encountered a bright orange saucer-shaped object. Appearing out of nowhere, the object flew parallel to the pair of bombers for more than five minutes. As it happened, the crews on both B-29s were combat veterans of World War II. They later said what they'd witnessed that night bore no resemblance to anything they'd ever seen before.

The air force's conclusion: The strange object was probably a "secret flare weapon" fielded by the communists.

In August 1952, near Sinuiju, North Korea, the crew of another B-29 bomber saw an orange cigar-shaped object streak by them at very high speed. The air force later claimed the crew had spotted a surface-to-air missile. The problem was, SAMs didn't come into service until 1954. What's more, the early versions were large, expensive, hard to move, hard to operate and built to protect major cities in the Soviet Union and the United States. It's extremely unlikely a SAM of any kind would be found in the wilds of North Korea in 1952.

On October 16, 1952, two pilots in a T-6 training aircraft were flying over the front lines in the eastern part of South Korea when they spotted a large silver ball, 25 feet in diameter, traveling at nearly 200 miles per hour. When the pilots turned to get a better look at it, the object accelerated to 800 miles per hour and disappeared out over the sea. Air force intelligence later concluded the object was "an enemy balloon."

Just after midnight on February 10, 1953, near Cho-do, North Korea, two U.S. Marines on guard duty spotted a large white object moving across the horizon. The object stopped, reversed direction, stopped again and then began moving back and forth across the sky, alternately flashing between red and white. A South Korean military officer stationed nearby also saw "a flying saucer" at the same time and same location in the sky. Eventually the air force ruled what all three men saw was "the planet Venus."

In February 1952, the Associated Press reported that the Far East Air Force headquarters in Tokyo was refusing to issue any definitive statement about flying saucers. The following month, famous newspaper columnist Drew Pearson wrote in the *Washington Post* that the Pentagon knew of more than two dozen flying saucer incidents over Korea that had been both seen by eyewitnesses *and* tracked on radar, but still they would not admit to them. The implication, and it was a good one, was that the military was covering something up.

This official reticence did not make the sightings go away, though. There were many dramatic incidents between 1950 and the 1953 armistice that just couldn't be explained— by anyone.

Another night in the fall of 1951 found a task force of U.S. Navy ships sailing off the coast of Korea.

This small fleet numbered fourteen vessels; its capital ship was a CVE, a modestly sized aircraft carrier. Each warship was equipped with its own radar system; each was monitoring the airspace around the task force, on the lookout for enemy aircraft.

Suddenly the carrier's radar systems lit up. An unidentified blip had appeared on its screens. Flying about a mile above the ocean's surface, some kind of unknown object was circling the fleet.

The aircraft carrier launched airplanes to confront the intruder. At that moment, everyone involved was certain this was a North Korean aircraft sent to spy on the task force as a prelude to an attack.

But though a number of carrier planes were quickly in the air, none of them could get a visual fix on the object. It was a dark night, but also a thick layer of clouds had blanketed the task force, making good visibility almost impossible.

What began as a scramble then became a desperate search. The object continued to circle the fourteen-ship fleet, never leaving its radar screens. But none of the carrier planes could get close enough to actually see the intruder.

This went on all night. But at one point, after another batch of carrier aircraft was launched to take up the hunt, the situation changed dramatically. The unknown object suddenly ceased orbiting the fleet and instead maneuvered behind one of the navy planes.

To the astonishment of all, the object began flying in close formation with this carrier plane, still unseen but right on its tail. It stayed this way for at least five minutes, and then the object abruptly sped off, leaving the area at a speed in excess of 1,000 miles per hour.

In all, the fleet's radars had tracked the object for more than seven hours.

Like the earlier case of the two huge saucers spotted by the trio of navy fighter-bombers, this incident could not be easily explained away. The initial suspicion was the object was a North Korean or Chinese MiG-15. (China had entered the war in the fall of 1950.) But like any jet fighter of the era, a MiG could stay airborne for only about two hours before its fuel began to run out. Yet, again, the navy ships had tracked the mystery object for more than *seven* hours. As aerial refueling had not yet been perfected, no military plane of *any* kind could stay in the air that long.

So, whatever was circling the task force that night, it wasn't a MiG.

A similar incident occurred on February 2, 1952. The U.S. Navy aircraft carrier USS *Philippine Sea* was sailing off the east coast of Korea when its radar operators picked up an unidentified incoming blip.

The object was 25 miles out from the carrier, flying at 52,000 feet, extremely high for any aircraft of the day. It was heading right for the carrier at high speed.

It was daytime, and what made this sighting unusual was that three observers on the carrier's deck had also sighted the object through long-range binoculars. Now being tracked both on radar and by human eyes, once the object was within 20 miles of the carrier, it was assumed not to be a friendly aircraft. A general alarm was sounded, and the carrier's crew rushed to their battle stations.

But just as this happened, the object performed a dramatic maneuver. It literally reversed direction in an instant and roared off at tremendous speed, fading from the carrier's radar screen at 110 miles away.

The carrier immediately reported the incident to the Commander of Naval Forces, Far East. Its message read, in part, that while tracking the object, the carrier's radar men had determined its speed went as high as 1,800 miles per hour, much faster than any aircraft of the day.

A few months later, a document detailing the incident was sent by the Commander of Naval Operations, Far East, to the Chief of Naval Operations. It was marked "Secret."

Among other things, it stated the encounter was probably the first instance of both a visual *and* radar contact of a "high-speed aerial target" made in the Korean theater.

Ground sightings of UFOs during Korea were not uncommon, either.

For instance, some of the most vicious battles of the conflict were fought at a place called Pork Chop Hill. Located northeast of Seoul along the so-called main line of resistance, U.S. troops engaged in a series of back and forth battles with communist Chinese forces in the spring and summer of 1953, all for what was essentially a worthless piece of ground. Just after one of these battles, ground observers spotted UFOs flying at speeds of more than 800 miles per hour over the area.

But nothing in the entire war can compare to what happened at a place called Chorwon.

Just as Keith Chester's *Strange Company* is considered the definitive book on "foo fighters," Dr. Richard Haines's book *Advanced Aerial Devices Reported During the Korean War* is the bible on UFO activity during the Korean conflict. The former NASA scientist gathered information on more than forty incidents involving UFOs and the U.S. military during the war, some of which have already been mentioned here.

But Haines also found and documented one of the most dramatic UFO incidents of any war, a rare "close encounter of the fifth kind," a chilling episode that showed a decidedly nonpacifist side of UFOs.

Early in the spring of 1951, U.S. Army private Francis Wall found himself in a bunker on the slope of a mountain near Chorwon, North Korea. Wall's unit was fighting the communists for control of a village below, and it was while they were shelling this village that something very strange happened.

"We suddenly noticed on our right-hand side what appeared to be a jack-o-lantern come wafting across the mountain," Wall told Haines years later in an interview for his book. "This thing continued on down to the village where our artillery bursts were exploding. It had an orange glow in the beginning. We further noticed it could get into the center of an airburst of artillery and yet remain unharmed."

Wall and his fellow soldiers watched the astonishing object for about thirty minutes. Then its disposition suddenly changed.

"This object approached us," Wall said. "It turned a brilliant blue-green and started pulsating."

Wall and his comrades became so alarmed, he asked his commanding officer for permission to fire at the object. His request was quickly granted.

"I fired at it with an M-1 rifle with armor-piercing bullets," Wall said. "And I hit it. It must have been metallic because you could hear the projectiles slamming into it. But why would a bullet damage this craft if the artillery rounds didn't? I don't know. But after I hit it, the object went wild. The light was going on and off. It was moving erratically from side to side, as though it might crash. Then, a sound—we had heard no sound previous to this—the sound of diesel locomotives revving up. That's the way this thing sounded."

Things quickly went from bad to worse for the shocked GIs.

"We were attacked," Wall stated. "We were swept by some form of ray. It was like a searchlight. You would feel a burning, tingling sensation all over your body [when it hit you], as though something were penetrating you.

"So the company commander hauled us into our bunkers. We didn't know what was going to happen. We were scared. These are underground dugouts where you have peepholes to look out to fire at the enemy. So, I'm in my bunker with another man. We're peeping out at this thing. It hovered over us for a while, lit up the whole area with its light, and then I saw it shoot off at a 45-degree angle, that quick, just there and gone."

Simply spotting a UFO is considered a close encounter of the first kind. Seeing a UFO and having some associated physical effects, like feeling heat from it, is considered a close encounter of the second kind. Third kind encounters involve observing beings with the UFO. Fourth kind encounters are when a human is abducted by those beings.

Private Wall's experience was a close encounter of the fifth kind (CE5). This is when a sort of two-way communication is established between the UFO and the humans that have encountered it. In this case, Walls fired at the Chorwon UFO, and it began a series of gyrations in response. As alarming as it was, two-way "communication" *was* established.

Even more astounding, Haines found other CE5 incidents years later in which the UFO in question acted in a very similar manner to the UFO at Chorwon, once it was "signaled." In at least one case this was accomplished by a hunter in the United States shooting at a UFO, just as Walls had done in Korea. Same means of "signaling," same gyrating reaction from the UFO, years later and a half a world away?

What does *that* tell us?

When the Chorwon UFO disappeared that day, it was not the end of it for Private Walls and his colleagues. Three days later, Walls's unit had to be evacuated from the battlefield. Roads were cut so the soldiers could be taken out by ambulance. Many were too weak to walk.

When army physicians examined them, they were all found to have extremely elevated white blood cell counts, a serious condition that doctors had no explanation for.

UFO sightings continued throughout the Korean War, but the U.S. Air Force never changed its stance in refusing to talk about them. One could say it was "adamant in its ignorance."

When the Korean War eventually came to an end, it was not by any clear-cut victory or peace treaty, but instead by a shaky armistice that, technically at least, is still in force today.

One quote, given by an air force spokesman during the conflict, seemed to say it all when it came to the subject of UFOs and the Korean War: "To affirm or deny that U.S. pilots were seeing UFOs over Korea would put the Air Force in the position of discussing UFOs. And we just will not do that."

15

Tales From the Cold War

One Spaceman's Journey...

In 1951, the U.S. Air Force's 525th Fighter-Bomber Squadron was based at Neubiberg, West Germany.

Located near Munich, the vast onetime Luftwaffe airfield was a short flight from the border of what was then communist-controlled Czechoslovakia. The 525th was there to patrol that hostile front line of the Cold War.

Tensions were high both in Europe and around the world in 1951. Germany was split in two, communist East staring down the democratic West. Russia now had atomic weapons. Its client state, North Korea, had invaded U.S. ally South Korea the year before, and no sooner had the United States gotten the upper hand in that war than a half million Red Chinese troops entered the fray, making the conflict even more bloody while threatening to turn Asia into a nuclear wasteland. In the early 1950s, all-out war with the Communist Bloc seemed inevitable.

The pilots of the 525th flew the F-86 Sabre jet; its communist adversaries just over the border were equipped with the MiG-15. These same two aircraft were battling each other on a daily basis high above Korea, half a world away.

Always on combat alert, the 525th was frequently scrambled whenever Soviet or Soviet-allied aircraft were detected too close to the border of West Germany.

So it was one particular day when a call came in that a virtual armada of unidentified aircraft had been spotted heading toward West Germany. The 525th was quickly airborne, its fighters climbing to meet what they were sure was an aerial onslaught of Russian MiGs.

But when the 525th Sabres reached their maximum altitude of 45,000 feet, their pilots discovered that the horde of bogeys were not Russian fighters. This air fleet was made up of metallic objects, shaped like saucers. And there were *lots* of them.

The objects were flying far too high for the Sabres to challenge them. So the 525th's pilots could do little more than watch as the swarm of UFOs passed over.

Flying one of those Sabres that day was a young second lieutenant named Gordon Cooper. As he would later tell it, streams of UFOs went over the 525th's base regularly for the next three days. Sometimes they were in groups of four; other times, in groups of as many as sixteen. They were almost always flying from east to west.

Again, Cooper and his colleagues could do little to stop them. Besides flying so high, the UFOs displayed high degrees of maneuverability. They would sometimes move at very high speed; other times they would hover motionless as the fighters of the 525th simply flew beneath them, helpless.

Finally, everyone realized that the 525th was wasting its time chasing the saucers; they eventually gave up trying to intercept them. Instead, the pilots would stay on the ground and use binoculars to watch the UFOs fly overhead.

The worst-case scenario—that the high-flying, incredibly maneuverable aircraft were of Soviet design—quickly faded. After a while it became the opinion of Cooper and just about anyone who'd seen them that these objects were not made in Russia, or China, or anywhere else on earth.

But even though word of the daily parade of UFOs was passed up the ladder to the highest levels of the Pentagon, no official investigation was ever undertaken to determine what they were. Once again, the U.S. military had its head planted firmly in the ground—or some other dark place.

Gordon Cooper gradually rose up the ranks of the air force, becoming an outstanding fighter pilot and then a test pilot. He was such a talented aviator that eight years later he would be selected as one of America's first astronauts. He would go on to hold the orbital record for the longest solo flight in a Mercury space capsule, circling the earth twenty-two times. A few years later, he was commander of an eight-day orbital mission in a Gemini capsule.

Cooper became a genuine American hero. Played by Dennis Quaid in the movie *The Right Stuff*, he went on to work for Disney and become a bestselling author.

But those strange days back at the beginning of the decade would not be his last experience with UFOs.

* * *

It's a peculiarity of history that the 1950s were considered a "peaceful" decade.

True, once the fighting in Korea had ended, the United States was not at war, at least not in the usual sense.

But a certain kind of conflict *was* taking place. It was a war of shadows fought mostly on secret battlegrounds. Though it never made the headlines, U.S. cargo planes converted to spy platforms and sent to fly close to Russia's borders were shot down with alarming frequency. Soviet spies were rife inside the United States, as evidenced by the Rudolph Abel atomic espionage ring and the execution of atomic spies Ethel and Julius Rosenberg. U.S. and Russian submarines stalked each other beneath the world's oceans. Huge armies on both sides of divided Europe were poised to strike on a moment's notice.

This was the "Cold War"—that state of affairs where East and West balanced themselves on the razor's edge of nuclear annihilation, their fingers always just millimeters away from pressing the button.

It was a strange time for other reasons, too. Literally *thousands* of UFOs were reported in the United States during the 1950s. It was a decade in which jet fighters chased UFOs and UFOs chased jet fighters, of near and actual midair collisions between aircraft and UFOs, of UFOs the size of aircraft carriers and of one actual aircraft carrier being haunted by UFOs. UFOs were seen watching the United States test its latest nuclear weapons, had made at least one jet fighter disappear and had buzzed the White House and the Capitol building—twice—forcing the president to instruct U.S. fighter pilots to shoot down any UFO that couldn't be "talked down."

There was even a UFO sighting above the very air base where the U.S. Air Force had once studied the flying saucer phenomenon.

Something was going on during the 1950s—something vastly mysterious and unknown and possibly even unknowable. The fifties might have been called a peaceful decade. But it could also be called the "Decade of the UFO."

While there were enough UFO incidents in those ten years to fill an encyclopedia, with thanks to the extensive, if sometimes dislocated, investigative work of the late, and some would say great, Captain Edward Ruppelt, U.S. Air Force, and taken primarily from his aforementioned book, *The Report on Unidentified Flying Objects*, what follows are some of the more unusual cases.

Comedy of Errors

Whether it was some kind of cosmic joke or an explicit attempt to send a message, one of the most remarkable UFO sightings of 1950 took place right over Wright-Patterson Air Force Base, the home of the U.S. Air Force's Air Technical Intelligence Center, the same people who at one time had claimed that flying saucers were real, only to be suppressed by Pentagon higher-ups.

Wright-Patterson is located in Dayton, Ohio, not far from what was the Dayton Municipal Airport. On March 8, 1950, a TWA airliner was beginning its landing approach to Dayton when its crew spotted a bright light off to the southeast.

The TWA pilot called the Dayton tower to inquire about the light; the air traffic controllers told him they already had the mysterious object in sight. The Dayton tower then called the operations hut of an Ohio Air National Guard unit based at the airport; they immediately scrambled an F-51 Mustang.

Meanwhile, the Dayton tower operators also called the nearby ATIC and told them what was happening right outside their front door.

The people at the ATIC hurried outside and saw the extremely bright light hovering right over their heads. Many of those investigators would later say the light was much brighter than any star they'd ever seen—and because it was midmorning, the chances this was a celestial body were practically nil anyway.

Some of the ATIC researchers rushed over to the Wright-Patterson radar laboratory, where they found an object had been picked up on the lab's radar in the same part of the sky where the mysterious light was hovering.

This blip was also showing up on the radar screen of the Ohio Air National Guard F-51, as well as another F-51 that had been scrambled from Wright-Patterson itself.

The pair of Mustangs were climbing together, and both pilots reported they could see the UFO and were intent on pursuing it. To this end, the lab's radar operator, a veteran master sergeant, gave both fighters a vector point and also linked their radios together.

The F-51s made it to 15,000 feet but then lost the UFO in the clouds. The pilots decided to continue the search, though. They put some space between them to avoid collision and continued climbing into the cumulus. But then their wings started icing up.

The radar operator back at Wright-Patterson was telling the pilots they were right underneath the UFO. But as the pilots couldn't see in the clouds and didn't want to slam into whatever the object was, they decided to cancel the pursuit.

The F-51s came back down to a safer altitude; moments later, the object began fading from the radar screen.

When the clouds cleared about an hour later, the UFO was gone.

What happened next was characteristic of how the U.S. Air Force would handle most UFO sightings in the coming decade.

A meeting was held at the ATIC shortly after the UFO sighting. While some ATIC radar experts were on hand, neither the F-51 pilots nor the master sergeant who'd actually run the radar intercept was at the meeting.

After some discussion, the ATIC experts, no longer charged with solving the UFO riddle, decided the sighting was caused by two simultaneous events. First, the bright light all the witnesses initially saw was the planet Venus. This, even though it was midmorning daytime.

And the radar return also seen by so many other people? That was caused by ice-laden clouds.

This dual conclusion seemed to be the result of two things: that Venus was located in the southeast sky at the time of the sighting—even though, again, it was midmorning and not nighttime, and that the F-51 pilots had reported ice on their wings when they went up through the clouds in search of the UFO.

So, case closed.

Except . . . neither the man who was running the radar intercept—a veteran of radar ops since before World War II—nor the F-51 pilots agreed with the report.

The radar expert was quoted as saying he knew ice clouds on a radar screen when he saw them. They came across as fuzzy, not solid as he had read the UFO that day.

Moreover, the F-51 pilots both said that as they climbed, they'd gotten a closer look at the object. One said it looked huge and metallic.

And just to double-check, this pilot searched for Venus in the same part of the sky the next day and it wasn't there—again, maybe because it was daytime.

But still, the air force considered the matter ended.

Atomic Spies in the Sky

Just down the street from the world-famous Las Vegas Strip, you can find what might be the most unusual military installation in the world.

It is Nellis Air Force Base. In addition to being so close to Sin City's main thoroughfare and serving as a huge installation for several air force fighter squadrons, Nellis also anchors the Nevada Test and Training Range, an enormous swath of restricted airspace larger than the state of Connecticut. Red Flag, the massive NATO simulated air warfare exercise, takes place there every year. Plus, about an hour northwest of Nellis is the infamous top secret spook base, Area 51.

Part of Nellis also serves as a major repository for nuclear weapons, and it's Nellis's longtime history with these kinds of armaments that resulted in one of the strangest UFO stories of the 1950s.

In 1951, the Atomic Energy Commission (AEC) established the Nevada Test Site. It was located 75 miles northwest of Nellis at a place called Yucca Flat. The AEC soon began detonating nuclear devices there, and airmen assigned to Nellis were routinely asked to provide security for the AEC testing site.

According to a report by Walter Webb, a consultant for MUFON, the highly respected UFO investigative network, on the morning of October 30 that same year, something very strange happened at Yucca Flat.

A group of Nellis airmen were acting as sentries for a test at the AEC site that day. The size of the explosion was to be between 10 and 20 kilotons, a substantial blast.

The airmen were in position just a few miles from ground zero. It was twenty minutes past dawn. The sun was at their backs, and the sky was clear.

Suddenly the airmen saw three silvery disks hovering close to where the bomb was about to go off.

The objects were shiny and reflected the early morning sunlight. They were described as having flat bottoms with a dome on top and were hanging in the air in a sort of triangle formation about a half mile high. They were making no sound.

On seeing the objects, the airmen called for their corporal, the senior man of the group. By the time the corporal arrived, a virtual fleet of UFOs had appeared, joining the original three. Suddenly there were eighteen UFOs hovering near the blast site. One airman said later the objects were arranged in a half dozen groups containing three UFOs each. They were stretched out horizontally.

The airmen observed the armada of disks for more than a minute. Then suddenly the UFOs turned upward and disappeared in an instant.

Once everyone caught their breath, the corporal said the

smart thing for them to do was forget what they'd seen. And this is what happened—the airmen involved never heard any mention of the incident again.

But years later, one of the men who was there finally revealed the sighting to MUFON, and it was his feeling that a lot more people had seen the UFOs that day than just his group of fellow servicemen. In fact, atomic tests were usually filmed by the AEC, using many cameras and shot from many angles. This means the appearance of the fleet of UFOs may have been recorded on film somewhere.

No such film has ever surfaced, though, and no explanation has ever been given for what happened that day at Yucca Flat.

But this incident would have a foreshadowing effect for years to come.

The Great Washington DC Saucer Flap

In July 1952, two of the most spectacular UFO sightings in history happened—and they took place right over Washington DC.

On two successive summer weekends, UFOs appeared in the sky over the nation's capital. They were tracked on radar, and seen by military and civilian pilots, as well as ordinary citizens in the surrounding area.

Fighter jets were scrambled, leading to a series of high-speed chases. At one point, four UFOs surrounded a fighter, forcing the pilot to call for help. Things got to the point where President Truman issued what might have been one of the most astonishing secret orders of all time, telling

U.S. military pilots to shoot down any UFO that couldn't be "talked down."

The U.S. military was so baffled, not only did they refuse to talk to the press at first, they even barred their own UFO investigators from looking into the matter.

It all started on July 19, a Saturday night.

Just a few minutes before midnight, seven objects popped up on radar screens inside the air traffic control (ATC) tower at Washington National Airport, now known as Reagan Airport. The radar indicated these objects were flying about 15 miles southwest of Washington, in an area well off the established flight paths and where no aircraft were supposed to be.

After first confirming their radars were working properly, the tower personnel contacted the airport's second radar center. The blips had shown up on its radar screens, too. What's more, people stationed at this second radar station could actually *see* the objects by looking out their windows.

When the objects started moving toward the White House and the Capitol building, the National tower called Andrews Air Force Base, about 10 miles away, and told their ATC personnel what was happening. Initially, the military personnel at Andrews saw nothing unusual. But no sooner had the first conversation ended than one of the Andrews ATC crew called the National tower back to say that not only were they now picking up the blips on their radar screen, but he, too, could actually see one of the objects.

As all this was going on, an airliner was waiting to take off from one of National's runways. Its pilot had seen a white object flash across the sky but had assumed it was a meteor. Yet just after takeoff, this pilot was informed by the National tower that UFOs were coming close to his airplane. The pilot responded that he could see six fast-moving objects, all without tails and white in color. The pilot had the strange objects in sight for nearly fifteen minutes, during which he was in constant radio contact with the National tower. The National controllers confirmed that whatever the airline pilot was seeing, they were seeing on their radar screens, too. And when the pilot reported that one of the objects had flown off at tremendous speed, it disappeared from radar screen at the National tower as well.

Finally, two jet fighters arrived on the scene. Runways at Andrews were under repair, so the fighters had to fly in from a base in Delaware. But just as soon as the airplanes showed up, all the UFOs suddenly disappeared. The fighters flew around for a while, trying to spot anything unusual, but they soon ran low on fuel and had to leave.

Just as the jets departed, though, incredibly, the UFOs returned. This led the ATC people in the National tower to believe that the UFOs were somehow listening in on the radio traffic between the tower and the jets, knowing when to come and go.

The sightings continued until around 5:30 A.M., when the UFOs finally left for good.

The following day, Americans awoke to headlines like: "Saucers Invade DC" and "Saucers Swarm Over Capital." The news immediately jammed the switchboards at both the White House and the Pentagon. People across the country feared the episode was just the start of some kind of UFO invasion of earth. Up to its neck with the fighting in Korea and other Cold War concerns, it's easy to imagine the quandary the U.S. military found itself in once news of the DC sightings became widespread.

Yet by pure coincidence, the U.S. Air Force's chief UFO investigator, Captain Edward Ruppelt of Project Blue Book, was in the Washington area that weekend. Project Blue Book was the successor to Project Grudge, the organization that was in charge of investigating aerial phenomena when the air force effectively slammed the door on any substantive UFO study back in 1949. Blue Book was started in 1951 as a revitalization of that study, in no small part because of the number of UFO sightings being made by military pilots fighting in Korea. And while never very robust in its methods, most UFO experts agree it was infinitely better than the days of Grudge.

Many of those same experts considered Captain Ruppelt to be the most open-minded military officer ever connected with investigating the UFO phenomena—though, on the other hand, that wasn't saying much. Interestingly enough, it was Ruppelt who in 1952 coined the term "UFO," feeling it took into account all strange things spotted in the sky, not just ones that were saucer shaped.

Having Ruppelt in town after the events of the weekend would have seemed the perfect situation for the air force then. A massive UFO sighting, one that had lasted for hours and had plenty of credible witnesses, had just taken place— and just by luck, the air force's number one UFO expert was close by. Common sense says a thorough, extensive investigation would have started immediately.

But that didn't happen.

Ruppelt didn't even know about the Saturday night sightings until two days after they happened—and even then he only found out by reading about them in the newspaper.

Immediately contacting his Pentagon superiors, Ruppelt was understandably anxious to begin investigating the sightings. Yet for reasons never fully determined, Ruppelt's own superiors refused to cooperate with him. They chose not to provide him with the barest essentials to start an inquiry, going so far as to deny him transportation, telling him if he wanted to visit Washington National Airport and Andrews Air Force Base, he'd have to take a taxi and pay for it himself.

Ruppelt was furious. He flew out of Washington and went back to Wright-Patterson Air Force Base where Project Blue Book was headquartered. What awaited him there was an avalanche of UFO sighting reports, from all across the country, spurred by the incident over DC.

One week later, another Saturday night, July 26, around 8 P.M., crewmembers of a National Airlines plane heading toward Washington DC suddenly spotted a group of unidentified objects flying above them.

The objects soon showed up on radar screens at National Airport and then Andrews Air Force Base. One of the Andrews's personnel once again got a visual on the objects.

The UFOs were back.

The press jumped on the story this time, but the Pentagon pushed back. A lower-tiered spokesman for Project Blue Book was at National Airport when reporters arrived. The first thing he did was to deny their request to take pictures of the objects on National's radar screens.

Within an hour, though, those same radar screens were

The Scandinavian ghost fliers of 1933–34 baffled the military and citizens alike.

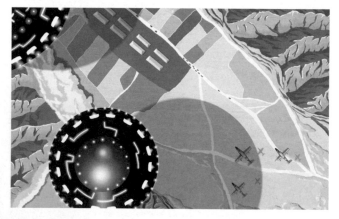

Allied aircrews saw many strange flying machines during World War II. They were eventually dubbed "foo fighters."

Although the U.S. Air Force claimed only "crackpots" saw flying saucers, dozens of UFO sightings by American pilots during the Korean War forced a change in policy.

America's "other" missile crisis: UFO incursions plagued U.S. ICBM bases throughout the 1960s and '70s.

Rumors persist that an American jet fighter shot down a UFO during the first Gulf War.

Why did UFOs haunt the USS *Franklin D. Roosevelt* throughout its three decades of service? Was it because the ship was the first U.S. Navy aircraft carrier to carry nuclear weapons?

Photo by U.S. Navy

Cruise missile technology wasn't perfected until the 1980s, and the first cruise missiles weren't used in combat until the 1990s. So why were cruise missiles like this spotted over Sweden in 1946?

Photo by U.S. Navy

A rare RB-47 shown in flight. Full of electronic countermeasures gear and other radar detection equipment, in 1957, one of these re-connaissance bombers was relentlessly stalked by a UFO over Louisiana and Texas for more than an hour.

Photo by U.S. Air Force

One of the first U.S. Air Force jet fighters to carry both a pilot and a radar operator, the F-94 Starfire was an unwitting player in several UFO incidents during the 1950s, including the especially baffling Haneda Case.

Photo by U.S. Air Force

detecting unidentified flying objects in all sectors around the airport. The ATC personnel watched dumbfounded as these UFOs performed seemingly impossible aerodynamic maneuvers, starting and stopping on a dime, reversing direction, sometimes moving at 100 miles per hour and the next moment, roaring off at 7,000 miles per hour.

By 11:30 P.M., two jet fighters had arrived, once again flying in from New Castle Air Force Base in Delaware. The fighters were directed toward the unknown objects. One fighter pilot saw nothing. But the second fighter spotted four white objects and took up the chase.

As the personnel in the National tower watched, this fighter pursued the four objects—until suddenly, the objects reversed direction. In an instant they'd surrounded the fighter.

Either nervous, perplexed or a little of both, the pilot asked the National tower what he should do. According to people who were there, his request was answered with stunned silence.

Seconds later, the four objects sped away.

By this time, the Blue Book liaison officer had arrived at the National tower. He had a phone conversation with the Washington office of the Weather Bureau and was told that there were some temperature inversion elements present above Washington DC. (Basically, different temperatures at different levels of the atmosphere can play tricks on radar screens.) But the Weather Bureau added that these effects were slight and not enough to cause the pickup of multiple blips on the National radar screen.

In other words, what the people in the National tower were seeing were solid objects.

Two more fighter jets appeared on the scene. As before, one pilot saw nothing while the other chased a white light before it, too, disappeared.

Then, just like the week before, the UFOs went away as soon as the sun came up.

No surprise this second round of sightings created a second round of bold-type headlines.

One such dramatic incident—UFOs buzzing the nation's capital—maybe could be explained away by weather phenomena, faulty equipment or overactive imaginations. But two?

Soon enough, Captain Ruppelt got a call from President Truman. The commander-in-chief wanted to know what was going on. Careful not to misspeak, Ruppelt took the safe route and explained that one reason for the radar sightings might be the temperature inversion theory.

But apparently Truman didn't buy it. On July 29 he issued his now-legendary "shoot down/talk down" order. Forgotten at the time, though, was that no U.S. jet fighter had ever been in a position yet to shoot down a UFO. And just how the pilots were supposed to "talk" one down was never addressed, either.

When word about the shoot down order got out to the public, the White House was once again inundated with calls from citizens across the country. Many argued that shooting at a UFO, a machine that obviously belonged to some higher technological power, was an insane course of action. They feared if we started shooting at UFOs, the UFOs might fry the earth to a crisp.

Typically, though, at the same time as the shoot down order was being given, the air force was also quoted as saying that UFOs were not a threat to the country's security nor did they believe they were under control of a higher intelligence, or any intelligence at all.

While it boggles the mind to think what kind of a reaction all this Pentagon bobbing and weaving would have gotten in a post-9/11 world, in 1952, the mixed messages only served to further confuse the American public on what had really happened.

So the U.S. Air Force decided to call a press conference. Held on July 29, it turned out to be the most crowded media event on a military matter since the end of World War II.

In attendance was a pair of high-ranking air force officers who argued that the DC sightings were one of either two things: shooting stars or something caused by temperature inversion. Basically the air force spokesmen said, take your pick.

The officers then reiterated that the contacts made by National Airport's radar weren't on solid objects and therefore were no threat to national security.

While Captain Ruppelt later wrote that the press conference succeeded in taking the pressure off the air force as far as the media was concerned, an avalanche of criticism from other quarters fell upon the Pentagon for their ineffectual explanations.

First of all, the Weather Bureau disputed what the air force had told the public. They said that the type of temperature inversion the air force had described would show itself as a steady line on a radarscope and not as a bunch of single targets, as were detected in the Washington area. When Captain Ruppelt checked with the Weather Bureau himself, he was told that the type of temperature inversion described by the Pentagon brass happened almost *every* night over Washington in the summer.

Then civilian eyewitnesses came forward, people who'd seen the objects flying over Washington at the same time the blips were showing up on radarscopes. Further research revealed that no one in the National or Andrews control towers on the nights in question agreed with the Pentagon's explanation, either. There was even a photo taken of the UFOs flying over the U.S. Capitol building!

Whether the general public realized it or not at the time, it was becoming clear that just as in the case of the Los Angeles UFO raid, the foo fighters, the ghost rockets and everything that had transpired since the Kenneth Arnold sighting, including incidents happening in parallel in the Korean Conflict, the U.S. military, despite all the denials and explanations, probably had no idea what UFOs were.

But at the same time, the U.S. military realized they had a big problem.

On a very basic level, the sheer volume of telephone calls that flooded the Pentagon during these kinds of UFO flaps was in itself a danger to national security.

The reasoning went, if an enemy of the United States wanted to sow confusion on the eve of an attack, all they had to do was somehow create a mass UFO sighting and the phone lines in and out of Washington would be horribly jammed. Panic would result, military commanders would be isolated and, in theory, the United States would be easy pickings.

Enter the CIA. Memos had bounced around the intelligence community after the Washington DC sightings, emphasizing this possibility of UFO-induced mass confusion. The result was that at the CIA's urging, a panel was created under the directorship of Howard Percy Robertson, a noted physicist. Its mission was to study the top cases of Project Blue Book and discern what was going on.

But sadly, it seems likely now that the Robertson panel had an agenda before it even started its work. Its members wound up discounting *all* of the Blue Book cases it had studied as far as them being threats to national security. The panel's conclusion was to recommend Project Blue Book stop investigating unexplained sightings and do more to *disprove* the existence of flying saucers. The air force brass made it so.

After that, Project Blue Book was mainly charged with releasing information to the public about UFO sightings that had "rational" explanations.

And what happened whenever they came up against a case they couldn't explain?

They just wouldn't talk about it.

UFO Chased, Shots Fired . . .

In that same summer of 1952, just about the same time as the flying saucer invasion of Washington DC, an air force jet interceptor, in another part of the country, actually fired on a UFO.

The location of the incident was kept secret by Project Blue Book's Captain Ruppelt when he wrote about it in his classic book, *The Report on Unidentified Flying Objects*. But still, he details the opening shots in what could have turned into exactly what all those people were warning the White House about: some kind of cataclysmic, one-sided interplanetary war.

As Ruppelt told the story, he was called to the unnamed U.S. air base and briefed on the sly by its intelligence officer about the UFO shooting incident. But he was also informed the base's commander had decided that instead of being defined by such a weird event happening on his turf, it was better to smear the pilot involved as a "psycho." And according to Ruppelt, that's exactly what happened.

It all started one morning when the base's radar picked up an unidentified flying object near the northeast part of the anonymous installation. The object was traveling at high speed—about Mach 1—when first detected. But just as suddenly, it reduced its velocity to a mere 100 miles per hour, a maneuver no aircraft in the world could do at the time.

Two of the base's fighter planes were scrambled with orders to intercept the object. The airplanes were F-86 Sabre jets, the air force's top fighters at the time. The base tower directed the Sabres toward the UFO, but as this was happening, the UFO began to fade off the base radar.

The control tower personnel were baffled. Had the UFO disappeared? Or was it flying so high—or so low—that it simply slipped off the radar screen?

The controllers decided the UFO was flying too high, so they instructed the F-86s to climb. Reaching 40,000 feet, the fighters found nothing—and by now the UFO had completely vanished from the base radar screens.

Perhaps the UFO had been flying too low then? The base told one of the F-86s to dive seven miles down to a tail-scraping altitude of 5,000 feet, while the other Sabre should take up station at 20,000 feet. The pilots complied.

On arriving at his prescribed altitude, the pilot who was ordered down to the deck saw a weird flash of light in front of him. Steering his F-86 in that direction, he spotted what at first looked like a weather balloon. But he knew this was impossible because the object was able to stay ahead of him—and he was flying at close to 700 miles per hour.

The pilot dove a little more, giving him additional speed but less altitude. The tactic worked, though, and he was soon just a half mile behind the mystery object. Finally, he got a close look at it and determined this was unquestionably no balloon. The pilot saw a definitive saucer shape; in his words, like a doughnut with no hole in the middle.

The pilot was soon on the UFO's tail—and the object was obviously doing its best to stay ahead of him. The pilot tried calling his wingman on the radio, but his message wouldn't go through. He tried calling the base's tower, but that message didn't get through, either. Meanwhile, he was only about 1,500 feet behind the object . . .

Suddenly, the object began to pick up speed. The F-86 pilot was in a quandary. What should he do? Ruppelt doesn't say whether this happened before or after President Truman's famous "UFO shoot down" order. But whatever the case, the pilot thought it was his duty to stop the intruder no matter what.

The F-86 was armed with six .50-caliber machine guns, firepower that could tear up another earthly aircraft with a few seconds' burst.

So, the pilot opened up on the UFO.

But whether he even hit it is impossible to know. Because an instant after he started firing, the UFO tremendously increased its speed, went nose up and quickly disappeared.

The pilot linked up with his wingman shortly afterward, and together they returned to base. That's when the smear campaign began.

No sooner had the two F-86s set down than the pilot in question was summoned before his direct superior, the squadron commander, and told to explain why he had fired his guns. After recounting what happened, the pilot was then called before the group commander, his overall superior officer. It was this officer, a colonel, who proceeded to trash the pilot's story.

First, he accused the F-86 pilot of going crazy. Then he claimed the man had fired his guns only as a lark and made up the UFO chase story to cover up his actions. According to Ruppelt, other pilots came to the man's defense, as did the base's flight surgeon. But the group commander was not swayed. He insisted the pilot was a psycho.

Ruppelt says the base intelligence officer wrote up a UFO sighting report but was ordered by the group commander not to send it to Project Blue Book.

Ignoring whatever importance such an incident might have meant to the overall UFO situation, which in 1952 was at a fever pitch, the group commander instead ordered all copies of the report destroyed.

The Haneda Case

One of the countless advantages of aviation technology is the use of aircraft for search and rescue (SAR).

If someone is lost at sea or in a wilderness, aircraft can cover many more miles in shorter amounts of time than people searching on the water's surface or on the ground. From a military point of view, highly trained search and rescue units are tasked with saving downed pilots or troops cut off from friendly forces.

Depending on the weather or the terrain, or who is controlling the ground below, there are a number of search patterns rescue aircraft can employ. The expanded square search, the sector search pattern, the parallel search pattern and the Williamson turn are all familiar to SAR personnel. These are proven methods of looking for something or someone from the air.

This aspect of search patterns became an interesting sidelight to yet another mysterious UFO sighting of the 1950s.

It happened over Haneda Air Force Base, a former U.S. Air Force installation that is now Tokyo International Airport. On August 5, 1952, just minutes before midnight, two air traffic control operators were walking to the base's tower to start their shift. Suddenly they spotted an incredibly bright light northeast of Tokyo Bay.

At first the controllers thought it was just an especially luminous star. But in the next moment they knew this was not the case, because by virtue of their jobs, they'd spent many hours looking up at the night sky—they knew a star when they saw one. As if to confirm this, they realized the light was actually moving; in fact it was coming right at them.

The men were soon up in the tower and, along with the personnel already on duty, began examining the mysterious light through powerful binoculars. It seemed to be illuminating the upper portion of a large, round dark shape, something much larger than the light itself.

This object was getting closer to the air base. It was also becoming more distinct, and now the controllers could see a second, but fainter, light on the bottom of the object.

Suddenly the UFO moved east, out of view of the control tower. But just as quickly, it appeared again. It stayed in sight for a few moments and then vanished again. But then it came back again.

What was going on? Why all these strange movements? A cargo plane was flying over Tokyo Bay nearby. The tower called the pilot and asked if he was seeing anything unusual. He replied no. But then the tower called a nearby radar station and asked if they had anything strange on their scopes. As it turned out, they did. And it was quickly determined that what the tower operators were seeing visually and the radar men were seeing electronically was the same thing.

Meanwhile the UFO continued acting peculiarly. It was moving back and forth above Tokyo Bay, sometimes hovering motionless, sometimes speeding up to more than 350 miles per hour. Throughout it all, while the radar men were watching the blip act this way on their screens, the tower personnel were watching the lighted object through their binoculars.

Shortly after midnight an F-94 interceptor scrambled

from a nearby base arrived over Haneda. The tower controllers directed the jet fighter to get behind the UFO. Seconds later the F-94's backseat radar man got a lock on the object. It was about three miles in front of the jet.

Now the tower personnel watched as both the F-94 and the UFO made a wide turn together. But the UFO got caught in the ground clutter—buildings and other obstructions that block radar beams—and the radar lock was broken.

At that point, the UFO started to accelerate away from the F-94; at the same moment, the tower operators lost sight of the object.

They called the F-94. Had they seen anything during the brief chase? The pilots responded they hadn't, besides the radar indication.

The fighter stayed around for another few minutes but found nothing else. It had to return to its base for fuel. As soon as it departed, though, the UFO came back.

The tower personnel saw it, and it was picked up by the radar station again. This time they kept it in sight for about two minutes when suddenly the UFO broke into three separate pieces. The three pieces left the area at high speed, and that ended the episode.

In all, the UFO had been in sight or tracked on radar for more than thirty minutes.

The Haneda sighting was so detailed, both visually and on radar, that it fascinated Captain Ruppelt, that is, back when his office was still nominally looking for the truth behind UFOs.

Ruppelt consulted with a group of Pentagon officers about whether UFOs appeared to be under intelligent control or simply flew through the air in a random helter-skelter fashion. This was an important question. If it could be shown that UFO flight patterns were random, then the UFO mystery might be deeper, but maybe not as interesting.

However, if it could be shown they *were* under intelligent control . . .

Ruppelt and the Pentagon officers discussed doing a study that would determine what kind of motion was used most often by UFOs. Random motion would be similar to a swarm of flying insects, with no pattern or purpose to their flight paths. But in a case like a flock of birds, where there are defined patterns to their movements, there's an ordered motion to them. The defined pattern indicates intelligent control.

In the Haneda incident, according to the witnesses, each turn the UFO took seemed deliberate, if unpredictable. As Ruppelt later studied the UFO's flight path from that night, basically moving back and forth over Tokyo Bay, it reminded him of search patterns that were used during World War II when SAR units we were looking for crews of downed airplanes. In fact, the only time the Haneda UFO strayed from its pattern was when the F-94 showed up.

Ruppelt came to the conclusion that doing an extensive motion study on UFO maneuvers was a great way to advance research into the phenomenon. He was anxious to pursue it.

But as usual, his superiors in the air force had other ideas. Those people in the Pentagon who could have actually approved and funded such a study turned him down cold. The promising idea died a quick and quiet death.

Later on, the Colorado Project, a skeptical UFO study effort with ties to the U.S. Air Force, determined the Haneda sighting was nothing more than false radar echoes caused by a temperature inversion layer.

The Haunted Carrier

History tells many tales of haunted sailing ships. The *Flying Dutchman*. The *Mary Celeste*. Even, in her day, the *Queen Mary* was thought to have ghosts.

But many believe the U.S. Navy once had a haunted ship—an aircraft carrier, in fact. And this ship's tormentors were not poltergeists. They were UFOs.

The USS *Franklin D. Roosevelt* was commissioned on October 27, 1945, shortly after the end of World War II. The following year, the ship was the first American aircraft carrier to launch and recover a jet aircraft. It also participated in what is still considered the longest flight ever from an aircraft carrier after a P2V Neptune naval bomber took off from its deck near Jacksonville, Florida, and landed in San Francisco the following day.

The *FDR* also took part in NATO's first ever naval war games—and that's when its bizarre connection to UFOs began.

The war games were called Operation Mainbrace; they took place over twelve days in September 1952. The U.S. Navy was the major contributor, but navies from the United Kingdom, Canada, Norway, Denmark, France, Belgium, Holland and Portugal also took part. The newly honed NATO fleet boasted more than 200 ships, 1,000 aircraft and 80,000 men.

The object of the war games was to repel an imaginary Soviet attack on Norway and Denmark; as such, the NATO armada was spread out over four large bodies of water: the Norwegian Sea, the Baltic Sea, the Barents Sea and the North Sea.

The centerpiece of this vast flotilla was the six participating U.S. Navy aircraft carriers, including the USS *Wasp*, the *Midway*, and the *FDR*.

The weirdness began on September 13, 1952. A Danish destroyer taking part in Mainbrace was sailing just south of Sweden when its commander and some of his crew spotted a triangular-shaped UFO streak overhead, traveling southeast. The witnesses said the object was moving at nearly 1,000 miles per hour.

On September 19, a British jet fighter returning to its home base in the UK arrived with a UFO on its tail. Witnesses on the ground described the object as a large rotating disk. Stopping in midair, the UFO lingered briefly over the airfield, then took off at tremendous speed, eventually disappearing to the southeast. The next day, three Danish Air Force officers spotted a shiny metallic disk streaking across the sky. They reported seeing it coming from the direction of the massive NATO fleet and then vanishing to the east.

That same day, September 20, a newspaper photographer who was on the *FDR* covering the war games at sea saw a group of crewmen looking at something overhead. It was a large spherical object moving extremely fast across the sky. The photographer quickly snapped off a few photos before the object disappeared.

On studying these photos, the carrier's intelligence officers decided the large spherical object had to be either a weather balloon—or something *else*.

The *FDR* quickly sent a message to all the ships in the

NATO fleet, asking if any had released a weather balloon. The answer that came back was unanimous—no. None of the ships had sent up a balloon.

The next day, September 21, six RAF pilots flying above the North Sea spotted a bright spherical object heading in the direction of the NATO fleet. The six jets started chasing it, but it quickly rocketed away.

The six planes returned to base, but just as they were landing, one pilot saw that the UFO was following him. He turned to chase it, but the UFO sped off.

On September 27 and 28, there were hundreds of UFO reports from West Germany, Denmark, and southern Sweden. Over Hamburg, a luminous object trailing a comet's tail was seen by many people for a long period of time. Other witnesses elsewhere in Germany saw three small UFOs orbiting a much larger UFO.

Once the war games were over, though, the UFOs went away.

The following year, the *FDR* went on maneuvers in the Caribbean. Having just gone through a refit at the navy shipyard in Portsmouth, New Hampshire, it was on its shakedown cruise. One night it was anchored off the U.S. Navy base at Guantánamo Bay, Cuba, the now infamous "Gitmo," when a UFO appeared above it.

The object was glowing with the intensity of a bright star. It began zooming around with fantastic quickness, but then would stop on a dime. It would hover, then streak off again, only to stop again seconds later. Many people on the *FDR*'s deck watched it until it disappeared in the light of the rising moon.

There was never any explanation for the object, and no official report was ever filed.

In the spring of 1956, after being refitted again and recommissioned at a shipyard in Washington State, the *FDR* was assigned a new home port at Mayport, Florida.

The ship was too massive to fit through the Panama Canal, so a trip around the tip of South America was necessary. On the way up the South Atlantic, the carrier stopped in Rio de Janeiro, Brazil, for a goodwill visit.

It was at anchor off Rio one night when two unknown aerial objects were spotted approaching the ship. The carrier's radars were immediately turned on, and word went through the crew that they were being stalked again. This time, by *two* UFOs.

Those who ran to the flight deck saw two large disks. They described them as one above the other, with a glowing light between the two. The objects were estimated at between 75 and 100 feet long.

They weren't moving, and there were a few hundred feet separating them. The ship's radar fixed them several miles from the carrier and about a half mile high. Each object had bright counterrotating lights ringing its middle.

Suddenly the top disk ejected a fiery object that fell into the lower object. After that, both disappeared at blinding speed. They went so fast, the ship's radar could not catch up with them.

Anyone in the ship's crew who witnessed the incident was later questioned by the navy and then told never to talk about it again.

*   *   *

In the fall of 1958, the *FDR* was back at Guantánamo Bay.

It was around 9 P.M. when a mysterious light appeared in the night sky and started heading right for the carrier.

Alerted that a UFO had been spotted, at least a couple dozen crewmen rushed to the flight deck. What they saw was a cigar-shaped object with a row of windows running through the middle. Some witnesses claimed they saw figures inside looking down at them. Others say they could feel heat coming from the object. Throughout it all, the craft did not make any noise.

The object remained hovering close to the ship for more than five minutes. Then it turned reddish orange—and then it was gone, leaving the area at very high speed.

Crewmen said that shortly afterward, the CIA arrived on the *FDR*. The reason the spooks gave for being on the carrier was to investigate illegal gambling on the ship.

In reality, they questioned any sailor who'd seen the UFO—and then warned everyone never to talk about the sighting again.

On October 2, 1962, the *FDR* was off the coast of Sardinia during one of its many tours of the Mediterranean.

At approximately 2 A.M., an aerial object was detected heading toward the ship.

The object was at the very edge of the ship's radarscopes, more than 500 miles out and 80,000 feet in altitude. But as the ship's radar operators watched in astonishment, the object descended nearly three miles in a matter of seconds and then just suddenly stopped.

Officers in the carrier's radar room confirmed the sighting, and the ship's captain was alerted. He immediately ordered the carrier to turn into the wind. In minutes, several F-4 Phantom fighter jets were catapulted off the deck with orders to confront the bogey. Once in the air, the Phantoms' pilots hit their afterburners and started to climb.

The fighters were soon close enough to pick up the UFO via their onboard radars, but this proved fruitless. In fact, the very moment they turned on their radars, the UFO disappeared from the *FDR*'s radar screens. The F-4s searched for more than twenty minutes but could not find anything. They were called back to the carrier.

But no sooner had the Phantoms landed and the carrier turned around to its previous course than the UFO blinked back onto the ship's radar screens. And this time it was right above the carrier, meaning it had traveled a distance of more than 500 miles in just a few minutes.

The UFO eventually disappeared for good. But when it came time to enter the details of the incident into the ship's log, the sailors responsible for that duty were told by their commanding officer not to enter anything.

The officer's words were: "This never happened."

Why did UFOs seem to target the *FDR*, among all the other aircraft carriers in the U.S. Navy?

There's only one clue: In 1950, the *FDR* was the first U.S. Navy carrier to deploy with nuclear weapons on board.

The *FDR* was decommissioned in 1977 and eventually scrapped. Years later, the ship's logs were thoroughly searched by UFO investigators, but no UFO reports were ever found.

The Disappearing Jet

On the evening of November 23, 1953, air traffic controllers at Truax Air Force Base in Wisconsin picked up a UFO on their radar screens.

The UFO had been detected flying near the Soo Locks, close to Sault Ste. Marie, Michigan. The Soo Locks is the channel that connects Lake Superior with the other Great Lakes.

North of the locks is Canada, so technically this channel constitutes the border of the United States. Because this was the Cold War era, the area was under constant monitoring, as were all border areas, by the Air Defense Command and was considered restricted airspace.

As the radar controllers at Truax continued tracking the UFO, a fighter plane was scrambled from Kinross Air Force Base in nearby Michigan. The aircraft was an F-89C Scorpion, a large, powerful jet for its day, capable of carrying both a pilot and a radar operator. This night, Lieutenant Felix Moncla was at the controls of the jet. Sitting behind him was his radar operator, Lieutenant Robert Wilson.

The UFO remained on the Truax radar as the F-89 approached, flying at 500 miles per hour at 8,000 feet. But once the fighter closed in on the object, the object abruptly changed course. Wilson could not get the UFO to show up on the F-89's radar, so Moncla had to rely on the Truax ground controllers to keep him on the UFO's tail.

The pursuit went on like this for about thirty minutes.

Finally, the F-89 was able to catch up to the UFO, which was now out over Lake Superior.

That's when the unbelievable happened.

With the ground radar operators watching, the two blips—one representing the F-89, the other the UFO—suddenly merged into one. The ground controllers were certain the fighter had simply overflown the UFO and would soon emerge on the other side. But this didn't happen.

Instead, the merged blip suddenly accelerated, leaving the radar screen completely.

The astonished ground controllers desperately tried radioing the F-89, but to no avail. Emergency rescue units were dispatched to search the F-89's last known position, which was approximately 160 miles northwest of the Soo Locks out over Lake Superior.

But nothing was found of the jet fighter.

The next day the *Chicago Tribune* ran the headline: "Jet, 2 Aboard, Vanishes Over Lake Superior."

The accompanying news story said the plane was on radar "until it merged with an object" but furnished no more details than that.

Pressed for an explanation in the days following the incident, the U.S. Air Force began its clumsy juggling act again. First, air force officials floated rumors that the pilot, Lieutenant Moncla, suffered from vertigo, was flying too low and probably crashed into the lake. In fact, this is what one air force spokesman told Moncla's widow. But it was pure speculation; plus Moncla had never been diagnosed with the inner-ear ailment.

Then the air force claimed the UFO had actually been a

propeller-driven Canadian Air Force DC-3 cargo plane, before suddenly changing its story again and stating a Canadian Air Force jet was to blame instead. Why the switch? Maybe because so many people had seen the UFO being tracked at 500 miles per hour, while a DC-3's top speed was just over 200 miles per hour.

Either way, the Canadian military responded that *none* of its aircraft—of any kind—had been over Lake Superior that night. Later, when Moncla's widow asked if her husband's remains could be recovered, the air force changed its story yet *again* and told her no, because now they claimed the F-89 had actually exploded at high altitude, meaning there were no remains.

As for the UFO and the F-89 "merging," another air force spokesman stated the F-89 and the UFO had actually been miles apart when the incident occurred, and something mechanical had brought down the jet. But of course, by using that line of reasoning, the air force was saying that its own radar operators—the people who were in charge of protecting America's borders from aerial attack—didn't know how to read a radar screen.

Sometime later, when UFO investigators wanted to look further into the incident, they discovered that the air force had deleted all references of the F-89's mission that night from the official records. In the files of Project Blue Book, the case is listed as an "accident."

The Incredible Gander Sighting

One of the most dramatic UFO incidents of the decade happened on February 10, 1956, out over the Atlantic Ocean.

At the time, the U.S. Navy had an airplane called the R7V-2 transport. A military version of the Lockheed Super Constellation, the top airliner of the time, it was a four-propeller aircraft with a distinctive tri-fin tail wing and the capacity to carry about ninety passengers or several tons of cargo.

This particular R7V-2 had left Keflavik, Iceland, after refueling and was heading for Gander Air Force Base in Newfoundland, with an eventual destination of the U. S. Navy air station at Patuxent River, Maryland.

The plane was flying at 19,000 feet, and the night was clear. The pilot was a U.S. Navy commander, a ten-year veteran who'd made the Atlantic crossing more than two hundred times. There were thirty U.S. military personnel on board the flight, including several aircrews. Most of these passengers were heading home after duty overseas.

About 90 miles from Gander, the pilot happened to look out on the ocean below, and instead of seeing complete darkness as usual, he saw a clutch of bright lights about 25 miles in front of him.

The pilot pointed this out to his copilot, who saw the lights, too. The pilot was sure the lights were coming from a village. But if that was true, then the plane must be over land, which meant it was wildly off course.

The plane's navigator disagreed, though; his instruments said they were directly on course. He suggested the lights might be a gathering of ships, possibly something to do with a special military operation.

The pilot then asked his radioman if he was picking up any chatter from ships nearby. His answer was no.

The other flight crews riding in back of the plane were

asked to come up to the cockpit. The pilot wanted them to see the lights, hoping one of them might have an answer to the mystery.

With these men in place, the pilot banked the large plane so everyone could get a better look. Suddenly, the lights below dimmed, to be replaced by several expanding colored rings.

As the aircrews watched in astonishment, one of these rings began getting bigger. In the next instant, everyone in the crowded cockpit realized this ring was not floating on the sea. It was actually rushing up toward the transport plane.

The pilot hastily pulled out of his turn and started climbing as fast as the plane would allow—but it was no use. This colored ring was on them in seconds. Only then was it clear the ring was actually the rim of a gigantic saucer-shaped craft that dwarfed the navy plane.

In fact, the saucer was nearly five times larger that the R7V-2—meaning it was at least 600 feet across and 30 feet thick.

The gigantic saucer very nearly collided with the transport plane. It had climbed almost five miles in less than eight seconds, moving somewhere between 2,000 and 2,200 miles per hour. But somehow, the craft's tremendous speed abruptly dissipated and a collision was avoided.

But then suddenly the giant saucer was riding off the plane's wing, not 300 feet away. The two craft flew like this for a short while. Then the monstrous saucer accelerated to tremendous speed, and in an instant, it was gone, disappearing into the night.

Regaining his composure, the pilot radioed Gander air base and asked if they had anything unusual on their radar.

Gander's radar station replied that they'd indeed picked up an unidentified blip but had failed to get it on the radio.

The pilot gave Gander a short version of what had just happened, then proceeded as quickly as possible to the air base. When the transport plane landed, several air force intelligence officers were on hand to greet it.

They immediately began questioning the crew, but it was obvious to the navy pilot from the start that their interrogators were not surprised the transport plane had come in contact with the huge saucer. In the two hours of extensive questioning that followed, the air force men wanted to know details like how close the saucer had come to the transport and was there any electrical interference noticed on the plane during the encounter; questions that indicated they'd been through this before.

The R7V-2 transport eventually made its way to its destination of Pax River air station. There, the passengers were interrogated again, this time by navy intelligence officers. Only then were the passengers free to go, told no doubt not to mention to anybody what had happened.

About a week after the incident, the transport plane's pilot got a call from a scientist working for a high level U.S. government agency. The scientist wanted to question the pilot about the saucer incident.

The navy had cleared the scientist to talk to the pilot, so the meeting was set up for the next day.

The scientist listened to the pilot's version of the encounter. Then, at the end of the session, the scientist took out a folder that contained photographs of UFOs.

He showed the photos to the pilot, asking if he recognized any of them. According to the pilot, the third photo showed exactly what he and his colleagues had seen over the Atlantic that night. The pilot was astonished that the scientist, and by extension, the U.S. government, had an exact photo of the object.

The pilot demanded the scientist tell him where he'd gotten the photo. His rationale was if the U.S. government had a photo of what he saw, then someone must know what it was.

But the scientist said nothing.

According to the pilot, the man just gathered up his photos and left, without another word.

When Worlds Collide . . .

On the morning of July 22, 1956, a U.S. Air Force Convair C-131D cargo plane piloted by Major Mervin Stenvers took off from Hamilton Air Force Base, California, heading to Albuquerque, New Mexico.

The plane climbed to 16,000 feet and leveled out. It was a clear day with good weather. The crew settled in for what promised to be a routine flight.

But soon after reaching a point about 30 miles north of Bakersfield, California, something went wrong.

Later on, a person on board the C-131 recalled that it felt like the airplane had hit a brick wall. One moment they'd been flying along smoothly; the next, the plane was shaking violently from the tail right up to the nose. An instant after that, the C-131 was plummeting straight down.

The plane fell about two miles before Major Stenvers, a man with thousands of flight hours under his belt, somehow got control back. He finally managed to level off, just a few seconds away from disaster.

Stenvers immediately radioed Bakersfield airport and, among other things, urgently requested clearance to make an emergency landing. Minutes later, the plane bounced into Bakersfield and rolled to a stop. The much-relieved crew climbed off the plane only to be greeted by something inexplicable. The airplane's tail was torn apart. Both the horizontal stabilizer and elevator were badly damaged. The tail structure itself was horribly bent. The crew was astonished. Considering the extent of the damage, that Stenvers had been able to get the plane down in one piece seemed miraculous.

The air force's official explanation was that rivets in the plane's tail had worked loose, causing the airstream to bend back the fuselage skin. In other words, metal fatigue. This had happened so quickly, the air force said, it led Stenvers and his crew to believe they'd hit something in midair.

But there was a problem with this. Subsequent investigation of the Convair C-131 airframe revealed no structural problems of that type. Indeed, at the time, there were hundreds of these planes flying as commercial airliners around the world. Had this been an inherent structural problem with this airframe, the plane, in all its variations, would have been grounded until a solution was found—and yet they weren't.

So what really happened?

Again, Stenvers and his copilot were certain they'd hit something in the air. But when local authorities searched for any wreckage on the ground in the vicinity of the incident, nothing was found.

Then came a report that a UFO had been spotted in the area shortly before the incident. Witnesses had seen an oval-shaped object flashing through the skies near Fresno, trailing a greenish light in its wake. Fresno is only about 50 miles away from where the incident happened.

So had the C-131 collided with a UFO?

Later on, one of the air force officers investigating the C-131 incident sent an anonymous report to UFO investigator Major Donald Keyhoe of the U.S. Marines. According to this source, whom Keyhoe trusted implicitly, shortly after regaining control of the C-131, Major Stenvers had indeed radioed Bakersfield, urgently requesting clearance to make an emergency landing. But he also told the ground control that his plane had been hit by a flying saucer.

His comments were never entered into the official account of the incident, and no follow-up investigation was ever done.

UFO Stalks Bomber

On the night of July 17, 1957, a U.S. Air Force RB-47H jet aircraft took off from Forbes Air Force Base in Topeka, Kansas, and headed south toward the Gulf of Mexico.

The six-man crew—two pilots, a navigator and three equipment monitors—had a busy night ahead of them. First, they were scheduled to do a gunnery drill over Texas. Then they would proceed to a navigation exercise over the open waters of the gulf, and finally, do an electronic countermeasures (ECM) exercise overland on the return trip to Topeka.

The RB-47 was a variant of the B-47 heavy bomber, the little brother of the B-52 Stratofortress. Normally manned by a crew of three, this particular model carried the three additional crewmembers needed to look after its sizable array of ECM gear. Located in stations at the rear of the airplane, these men were known as EWOs, or electronic warfare officers.

The equipment jammed inside the big six-engine plane could best be described as "antiradar" gear. Designed to detect electromagnetic radiation coming from sources on the ground, the RB-47 had the means to pinpoint enemy radar stations that other U.S. aircraft could then bomb and destroy. This particular plane and crew were soon to be deployed to Germany and the front line of the Cold War, thus the need for the training mission.

By 4 A.M., the aircraft crew had finished their gunnery exercise and their open-water navigation training. The big plane was now turning back toward the coast, intent on making landfall somewhere above Gulfport, Mississippi. That's when one of its EWOs detected a bizarre signal on his ECM equipment. It indicated something was following the airplane.

This was odd because the signal was of a type normally emitted by radar ground stations. Yet it was coming from an airborne source out over the Gulf.

The only explanation was the equipment was malfunctioning. But then as the EWO watched, the signal's source came right up on the plane—and according to his scope, began to fly a ring around it.

The EWO was astonished. The RB-47 was traveling at 500 miles per hour, nearly as fast as the fastest jet fighters of the day. What could fly a ring around the big bomber?

It was *so* peculiar, the EWO became convinced something was wrong with his gear and said nothing to the rest of the crew. As the plane flew north, the signal faded from his scope.

Time passed. The plane made its uneventful preassigned turn over Mississippi. The task now was to work the aircraft's ECM antiradar detection gear, using air force radar units on the ground as simulated targets.

Just as this part of the mission was about to begin, though, the RB-47's pilot saw a bright light off to his left. It was flying around 34,000 feet, the same altitude as his aircraft.

Thinking it was another airplane straying into their flight path, the pilot ordered the crew to prepare for evasive action. But before the crew could react, the bright light flashed by the nose of the aircraft at tremendous speed— and then blinked out.

Recovering quickly from the near miss, the pilot hastily explained to the crew what had just happened. That's when the EWO revealed the odd signal he'd picked up a short time before.

It was now about 4:10 A.M. CST, and the plane was somewhere over Louisiana. The EWO rechecked his equipment and discovered a signal in the same location as the pilot had seen the bright light before it blinked out. The ECM equipment was checked again, and all of it was found in good working order. This confirmed that the signal was not coming from ground-based radar.

That's when the plane's crew realized that the signal's source—whatever it was—was flying alongside the RB-47, keeping pace with it, even as the plane was still flying at 500 miles per hour.

* * *

The RB-47 was soon back over Texas.

Again the pilot spotted an extremely bright light in front of the aircraft and about a mile below. Then the EWOs reported seeing two signals, and sure enough, the pilot and copilot saw red lights in those locations. The pilot contacted a radar station near Duncansville, Texas, and reported what was going on. When he gave the radar station personnel the position of the mysterious lights, they confirmed they were picking up radar blips exactly where the RB-47 crew said the blips would be.

Deciding they'd had enough of this, the RB-47 pilot requested permission from the Duncansville station to pursue the lights. Permission was granted—and the chase was on.

The RB-47 set off toward one of the lights. Just a few seconds into the pursuit, though, the light stopped in mid-air, causing the jet to overshoot it. Moments later, the light blinked out. When it did, it also disappeared from the RB-47's radar, as well as that of the radar station on the ground.

The RB-47 pilot went into a steep turn, and the light suddenly blinked back on again—along with radar indications on the plane's scope and those below. Now the RB-47 found itself only about five miles away from the UFO. But suddenly the object dropped three miles down to 15,000 feet and disappeared again, both visually and from radar.

At this point, low on fuel, the RB-47 had to return to its original course. The airplane picked up a signal two minutes later, and the pilots saw one of the lights once more. Passing over Oklahoma, this signal's source took up station behind the bomber again. It finally vanished just as the

RB-47 was passing over Oklahoma City. In all, the stalking had lasted more than an hour.

Though it couldn't explain how the bomber's sophisticated equipment had tracked something close by in the air during the flight, or how that something managed to blink on and off of at least two tracking radar screens, *or* that the RB-47's pilots had actually *seen* not one but *two* bright lights in the sky and had actually given pursuit, Project Blue Book nevertheless said later that the sightings were caused by an ordinary jet airliner.

A Circle Is Completed

On the morning of May 3, 1957, a film crew at Edwards Air Force Base was tasked with filming a new piece of equipment near one of the base's runways. The film crew consisted of two enlisted men. Both were trained photographers and were experienced at shooting pictures at the vast air base.

Located in the desert on the far eastern edge of Los Angeles County, Edwards was then, and still is today, a mecca for America's military pilots. Its official name is the Air Force Flight Test Center, and as such it is the gathering place for this country's test pilots, the elite among America's air warriors.

Many of the U.S. military's experimental aircraft have been flight-tested there over the years. Because the air base is located next to an enormous dry lake bed, its runways literally extend for miles, a necessity when flying new, advanced and unpredictable airframes.

Edwards is also a highly restricted place. All of its activities are classified. Security breaches there are considered on the same level as those at Area 51, several hundred miles to the northeast in the Nevada desert. In fact, technically speaking, Area 51 is considered an extension of Edwards Air Force Base.

This day, the two enlisted men were filming a precision landing device called an Askania system. It consisted of a specialized camera designed to take one frame per second, images that would be used later to study aircraft landing characteristics.

They were equipped with a movie camera as well as a regular still camera.

They began work at 8 A.M.

Later that morning, the two men, out of breath and extremely anxious, rushed in to see their commanding officer.

They'd just seen a flying saucer out on the runway—this is what they told their superior. The craft had flown right over their heads, had landed about 150 feet away from them, and when they tried to approach it, it took off at great speed. The object was indeed saucer shaped, was silver metallic and had landed on three extended gears.

Given that these men were photographers, the officer's first question was obvious. "Did you get any pictures?" he asked.

They replied: "Yes, sir. We were shooting the whole time."

The officer told the men to develop the film immediately. In the meantime the officer called a special number at the Pentagon used by the military for occasions such as this. The officer's first conversation was with another captain.

He was then passed on to a colonel who passed him on to a general. The general ordered him to develop the film but not to make any copies. He was then to put the film into a secure pouch and have it flown immediately to Washington DC on the Edwards base commander's plane.

The officer did what the general ordered, but not before looking at the still camera's negatives. What he saw astonished him. The photos were clear, crisp and in focus—and indeed, they showed the object landing, at rest and taking off again. He didn't look at the motion-picture film—but he didn't have to. He knew he was looking at a flying saucer.

And that was ironic, to say he least, because this was not the officer's first brush with UFOs.

The officer was Gordon Cooper, now a captain and a test pilot, and just a couple of years away from being selected as one of America's first astronauts.

What he'd seen up close in the photos was pretty much what he'd seen flying so high over West Germany back in 1951.

The circle was complete—or so it seemed.

Cooper said later that once the photos and film reached Washington, he was sure there would be a huge investigation and that he'd be asked about everything he knew.

But that investigation never materialized. Despite the fact that there was now photographic evidence of a flying saucer landing, in the middle of a highly classified installation no less, the air force never did anything about it. There was no follow-up. In fact, no one in the military ever mentioned it to Cooper again.

To his dying day—October 4, 2004—Gordon Cooper, test pilot, astronaut and American hero, not just suspected, but actually *knew*, like *hundreds* of other U.S. military pilots—pilots who'd been told they were chasing temperature inversions, 800-mile-per-hour balloons, off-course airliners and the planet Venus—knew, that UFOs existed, and that throughout the 1950s the government they'd devoted their lives to had gone to great lengths to cover them up.

PART SIX

The 1960s and 1970s

16

The Great ICBM Flap

In autumn of 1962, the Soviet Union secretly installed nuclear-armed missiles on the communist-controlled island of Cuba, just 90 miles off the tip of Florida.

The missiles were soon detected by American spy planes, and the U.S. president at the time, John F. Kennedy, demanded the Soviets remove them or risk an all-out nuclear war.

For two weeks the world held its collective breath, fully aware that a massive nuclear exchange would end most, if not all, life on Earth.

The crisis eased at the end of October when the Soviets agreed to dismantle their missile sites. But the whole frightening episode gave the American public a harsh education on what nuclear brinkmanship was all about and how at the time, the United States and Russia alone had enough atomic weapons, including intercontinental ballistic missiles (ICBMs), to destroy the planet many times over.

The crisis played out on TV, on radio and in newspapers. Every American citizen knew what was happening hour by hour, if not minute by minute. Those two weeks in October 1962 were unparalleled for creating fear and uncertainty around the world.

But very few people know that starting right around the same time in the early 1960s, the United States had *another* nuclear missile crisis. This one involved an extremely mysterious entity that caused dozens of security breaches at U.S. ICBM sites, at times shutting down their launch mechanisms, at times starting launch sequences and, by some reports, at times even *breaking into* ICBM launch silos, which are among the most guarded, most military-sensitive installations on earth.

And no, these weren't the Russians doing this. This secret nuclear crisis was caused by the mysterious entity we've all come to know as UFOs.

During the Cold War, the most powerful section of the U.S. military, and likely the most powerful body on earth, was the U.S. Air Force's Strategic Air Command.

More readily known as SAC, it controlled all of the air force's nuclear-armed bombers, plus all of America's ICBMs, those hundreds of nuclear-tipped missiles that would be launched should World War III break out. It was SAC's collective fingers that were resting on the doomsday button.

SAC's main headquarters was located at Offutt Air Force Base near Omaha, Nebraska. (SAC's replacement, the U.S. Strategic Command, is headquartered there still.)

Then or now, there is probably no other U.S. military facility as crucial to America's national security as Offutt.

That's why what happened there in September 1958 was both baffling and frightening—and a harbinger of some very unsettling things to come.

It was September 8, just after sunset, and the sky above Offutt was clear.

Several people noticed what at first appeared to be a harmless vapor trail high above the base. But as the witnesses studied it further, the vapor trail began displaying characteristics not found in leftover contrails. It became extremely bright, like a magnesium flare, in one person's description. As the light grew in intensity, more people on the ground became aware something strange was happening.

One witness called the base's control tower. As he talked to the ATC personnel, the light high above them began changing color. Suddenly it was reddish orange. And what had previously been of undefined vaporous appearance now took on the distinct form of a cigar-shaped object standing on its head. The witnesses below, many of them veteran pilots of World War II and Korea, were stunned.

But the sighting only got stranger. From the bottom end of the object came a mass of small black flecks, like a swarm of bugs, a description used at least once during a World War II foo fighter episode. These things poured out of the object for more than a minute, flying off in every direction before they all disappeared.

Then the object itself began moving. First, it changed its attitude, swinging around 45 degrees to strictly horizontal.

Then it began slowly drifting west. The witnesses watched this transformation for about five minutes before the object changed attitude again, returning almost but not quite to its previous upright position.

Then the object simply faded away.

Again, those watching on the ground were just bewildered. One officer gave a detailed report of the incident to higher brass and was told that he'd be hearing from ATIC, as in Project Blue Book, within forty-eight hours.

But that call never came.

For the most part, the missiles in America's top secret ICBM bases in the 1960s were known as Minutemen. Each was capable of carrying 1.2 megatons of nuclear explosive, meaning just one Minuteman contained fifty times the explosive power of the atomic bomb dropped on Hiroshima.

Minuteman missiles were primarily deployed to bases throughout the geographical center of America, and to a degree, they were concentrated in Missouri, Montana, North Dakota, South Dakota and Wyoming. Each base commanded between 150 and 200 missiles, all of them housed in separate silos built deep in the ground and constructed of heavily reinforced concrete.

Each missile silo was connected to a launch control facility. These underground control rooms were staffed twenty-four hours a day. They had their own guards as well as mobile security teams.

To increase survivability, the missile silos were spread out over vast open areas, each silo usually located many miles from any other. For example, missiles controlled by

Warren Air Force Base, headquartered near Cheyenne, Wyoming, were deployed over 9,600 square miles; some of them spilled over into western Nebraska and northern Colorado in addition to those in eastern Wyoming.

This was the makeup of America's massive long-range nuclear weapon delivery system. Situated mostly on isolated flatlands and prairies, well away from population centers, each missile was aimed at a Soviet (or Soviet-allied) target, a thirty-minute transpolar flight away from igniting Armageddon.

There were almost a dozen major ICBM bases in all—and by early 1967, every one of them had reported UFO incidents.

Unlike most of the sightings of foo fighters during World War II, the incidents at America's ICBM bases were reported by people on the ground, not by the crews of aircraft in flight. So, what these witnesses described could not have been the result of the distortion that can occur when two objects are in motion relative to each other, or engine exhausts from another aircraft, or meteorological-induced electrical discharges, or flak, or some enemy's secret wonder weapon or any other kind of misleading aerial phenomena.

This was something else.

That UFOs would start appearing over America's nuclear facilities probably shouldn't have come as much of a surprise to the U.S. military.

No less than four times between 1945 and 1952, UFOs were reported hovering over the Hanford Engineering Works, in Hanford, Washington, the site of America's first nuclear reactor. One report in 1945 said the interloping UFO was the size of three aircraft carriers put together. UFOs had been reported over other U.S. nuclear facilities as well, such as Oak Ridge, Tennessee, and Los Alamos, New Mexico.

But these particular UFO incidents occurred at reactors. The UFO haunting of America's ICBM bases was a different case because these places housed nuclear *weapons*.

With thanks to Robert Hastings, author of the definitive *UFOs and Nukes: Extraordinary Encounters at Nuclear Weapons Sites*, the National UFO Reporting Center (www .nuforc.org) and NICAP, what follows are some of the most unusual and frightening accounts of what happened to a large part of America's ground-based nuclear arsenal in the 1960s and '70s.

Something almost inconceivably strange.

Something that's never been explained.

The Scariness Begins . . .

Like the foo fighters of World War II, the ghost fliers of 1933–34 and other unusual UFO episodes, this one began with a single odd incident.

Hastings tells us it happened in the summer of 1962. A worker at a yet-to-be-completed ICBM base near Oracle, Arizona, spotted a very bright light hovering over a half-built missile silo. The silo was empty at the time, but nearby Davis-Monthan Air Force Base was contacted anyway. Two jet interceptors were sent to the scene, but the light disappeared as soon as they arrived. Yet no sooner had the jets departed than the light reappeared.

It was seen hovering over the unfinished silo for a short while longer before leaving for good.

The Walker Sightings, 1963—64

Located in southeast New Mexico, Walker Air Force Base received its first ICBM in early 1962. Within a year, personnel assigned to the vast facility were reporting UFOs either hovering or moving very fast over their missile sites.

According to Hastings, one officer assigned to Walker at the time recalled up to nine occasions when guards reported seeing UFOs shining bright lights down onto missile silos. Though these incidents were reported to higher authorities, the air force brass did nothing about them.

In fact, right from the beginning of the odd goings-on at Walker, the air force seemed either uninterested, reluctant or under orders not to investigate anything having to do with UFO sightings.

This baffling lack of interest was confirmed by another officer assigned to Walker, who said in the fall of 1964, security personnel reported seeing an extremely bright light repeatedly hovering over one particular missile site, then racing away, returning, and hovering again. Many people witnessed this inexplicable behavior, yet the air force never debriefed any of them.

Still another airman at Walker contacted his superiors when he saw two starlike objects moving over his launch facility. As it turned out, the objects were already being tracked on Walker's radar, and two jet fighters from a nearby air base had been scrambled to intercept them. Witnesses even saw the jets streak toward the mysterious objects only to see the

UFOs accelerate to an incredible speed and disappear from sight. But later reports said that Walker's commanders not only denied that anyone saw UFOs that night, they even denied they'd requested any fighters to intercept them.

But then one missile technician at Walker had an encounter with a UFO that was so up close and personal, it was hard to ignore.

This man was working deep inside one of the missile silos one night when a guard up top reported that strange lights had appeared outside the silo's perimeter. The technician emerged from the underground facility to see that what he later described as a "noiseless, brilliant and seemingly dimensionless object" had landed on the ground close to the missile silo.

Flashlights in hand, the technician and the guard slowly approached the strange object, only to have it suddenly disappear, then reappear briefly 30 feet away before vanishing for good.

The technician later told his story to a member of the U.S. Air Force's Office of Special Investigations, the somewhat shadowy OSI. But the man was never told whether a formal report was ever filed or not.

So many strange things had happened at Walker Air Force Base during 1963–64 that one worker finally contacted NICAP, the National Investigations Committee on Aerial Phenomena. In a letter written in December 1964, the worker said the UFO sightings at the base had become so numerous, many guards were too frightened to go on duty. Yet the air force insisted that everything related to the sightings should be considered "top secret."

Even more disturbing, at least for some hard-core true believers, is that this worker also told NICAP that one missile site at Walker in particular had endured many recurring UFO sightings.

That site was Site 8, located just south of Roswell, New Mexico. In fact, before it was renamed for Kenneth Walker, a World War II Medal of Honor recipient, Walker AFB was known by another name: Roswell Army Airfield.

The Warren Sightings

Warren Air Force Base, located about three miles west of Cheyenne, Wyoming, is one of the oldest military bases in America, having started life as a frontier fort in 1867. It is also one of the largest nuclear missile bases in the world.

In 1965, multiple UFO sightings were reported at the base. On the night of August 1 alone, there were eleven reports about strange objects flying over the huge missile facility; one of these reports was made by the base commander himself. Some witnesses that night saw single objects; others saw up to nine UFOs. Many of these sightings were corroborated by different people seeing the same things at the same time, just from different vantage points.

On another occasion, one of the base's security policemen saw eight brilliant lights hovering over an isolated missile silo. The lights were grouped in pairs and were motionless, at least at first. Then one of the lights began to move among the others, apparently going from pair to pair. The policeman watched this bizarre activity for several minutes before reporting it to his commander.

The policeman was told that NORAD (the all-seeing North American Aerospace Defense Command, located near Colorado Springs, Colorado) had notified the base that its radars had been tracking the eight unknowns as well, but before anything else could happen, the UFOs disappeared.

A week later, another strange incident was reported at the same missile silo. In this case, the site's security team was sitting in a camper-type vehicle parked near the silo. Without warning, the vehicle began to shake violently. The security men looked out of the window and saw a bright white light hovering directly overhead. The shaking lasted until the light above disappeared.

The rash of sightings at Warren Air Force Base continued for almost a month. During that time, ranchers in that part of Wyoming also reported seeing UFOs, and some even claimed that they had cattle missing. An airman testified that one night, when the base police tried to preserve a suspected UFO landing site, they were ordered by base higher-ups not to do so.

From all reports, the U.S. Air Force brass at Warren simply ignored the incidents.

The Whiteman 1966 Sighting

Whiteman Air Force Base is located about 70 miles east of Kansas City, Missouri. Formerly a glider training base, today it is the home of the B-2 Spirit stealth bomber. In the late 1990s, B-2s from Whiteman flew nonstop round-trip bombing runs to Yugoslavia during the Kosovo crisis. They did the same thing a few years later in support of the war in Afghanistan and the U.S. invasion of Iraq.

During the 1960s, though, Whiteman housed a vast ICBM complex, containing up to 150 missiles. It was there that one of the scariest, most inexplicable UFO incursions occurred.

According to a report given to NUFORC, it started around 9 P.M. on the night of June 16, 1966, when the base's control tower personnel detected a saucer-shaped object flying over the southernmost part of the missile complex. The object's flight path eventually took it over one of the base's ICBM launch silos. When it passed over this site, the missile inside the silo lost all electrical power. This very serious condition is known as "going off alert status."

The electricity returned to the missile silo as soon as the UFO left the immediate area. But then the same thing happened to the next silo the object came to. The power went out, coming back on as soon as the UFO had passed over. Then it happened to the next silo, and the next—and the next.

Incredibly, the UFO flew around the Whiteman complex for the following two hours, killing power in *all* 150 missiles controlled by the base, all while these missiles were armed. Finally, the object flew off to the north and disappeared again.

The Ellsworth Intruder

Ellsworth Air Force Base is located close to Rapid City, South Dakota, in the southwest corner of the state.

Once a training site for B-17 Flying Fortresses, these days Ellsworth is home to a wing of B-1B Lancer bombers. But in the 1960s, the sprawling facility was an ICBM base, and it was there, not two weeks after the bizarre happenings at Whiteman, that another incredibly strange UFO incursion took place.

As Hastings reports in *UFOs and Nukes*, on the night of June 25, 1966, two technicians were sent to one of the base's missile silos, code-named Juliet-3. All electrical power to the silo's ICBM had mysteriously failed. The technicians corrected the problem and completed the missile's automatic restart procedure. Returning aboveground, though, the technicians heard via their radio that a security alarm had gone off at another silo nearby. Code-named Juliet-5, its missile had lost all power, too.

As they continued to monitor the radio transmission, the two technicians soon heard the excited voices of the security team sent to investigate the Juliet-5 alarm. They were shouting that a strange object was resting on the ground inside the silo's security fence. The security team leader described the object as a metal sphere supported by a tripod-style landing gear.

It sounded crazy, but from their location at Juliet-3, the two technicians and a security guard who'd accompanied them could see an intense glow coming from Juliet-5, four miles away.

As the astonishing radio transmission continued, the technicians heard the Juliet-5 team leader twice refuse orders to approach the mysterious object, instead asking the base's top security officer for permission to fire at it. Clearly under stress—the ICBM inside the Juliet-5 silo was armed and targeted at the Soviet Union—this officer ordered the security team not to use their weapons until the situation had been clarified. He then reassured the security team that a helicopter was on its way to the Juliet-5 site.

Subsequent radio transmissions made it clear that Ellsworth's base commander, wing commander and missile maintenance commander, among others, were on board the helicopter heading for Juliet-5.

Such a collection of upper brass being in one place at

one time was extremely rare. For them all to be put on a helicopter, at night, when rotary-wing flying wasn't the safest, was almost unheard of.

But just as the helicopter was approaching Juliet-5, the security team leader was heard shouting that the mysterious object was leaving. At that exact moment, the three witnesses at Juliet-3 saw a bright beam of light rise up from Juliet-5 and fly off at an incredible speed.

The helicopter landed moments later, and its high-ranking passengers entered the sealed-off area. They saw three indentations in the ground, each about 25 feet apart, forming a triangle. The marks were just what would be expected from the landing gear the security team leader had described.

And at that moment, to everyone's amazement, the electricity at Juliet-5 suddenly came back on, restored as mysteriously as it had been lost.

When the two technicians and the security man who had followed the incident from Juliet-3 returned to base ops, they were questioned extensively about what they'd seen and heard.

The security guard admitted he'd overheard the radio chatter. But knowing that others had been punished for talking about UFOs, the techs lied, saying they'd been underground when it all happened and had witnessed nothing unusual.

The three men were questioned again the next day, this time in the presence of an unidentified civilian, most likely a member of the air force's OSI.

The techs stuck to their story. The security man stuck to his. Nothing happened to the techs, but neither saw the security guard again.

The Malmstrom Shutdowns

According to several published accounts, including one by Hastings, Malmstrom Air Force Base, near Great Falls, Montana, was the next target of the UFO incursions.

In early February 1967, some local residents saw strange objects flashing across the sky. These would be a prelude to what happened next.

One night in mid-February, a Malmstrom security officer took a call from an airman doing a routine check of one of the base's isolated launch facilities.

The airman was frightened. He told the officer that he was looking at a huge shining object hovering over the missile silo. The officer didn't believe the airman at first—it just sounded too fantastic. The airman's repeated pleas finally convinced the officer, though. He, in turn, notified Malmstrom's command post—but, incredibly, he was told that the command post no longer took "those kinds of reports."

The only other action the officer could think of was to authorize the airman to fire on the UFO. While the airman appreciated the officer's authorization, he remarked that considering what he was looking at, shooting it wouldn't do any good.

The UFO flew away shortly afterward.

A few weeks later, in the early morning of March 16, a blaring alarm went off across Malmstrom. One of the facility's ICBMs had suddenly gone off-line and was now inoperable.

Command post officers phoned the affected missile site. The prevailing thought was that a maintenance crew had caused the malfunction. Instead, the security guard at the site responded that no maintenance had been performed at the silo that morning—but people *had* seen a UFO hovering over the site.

The command officers did not take this report seriously—but then other warnings started coming in. More missiles were shutting down, one after the other. In just a few seconds, ten of Malmstrom's ICBMs were inoperable.

This was serious. A large part of America's national security depended on the capability of these missiles—and at the moment, they were useless.

The command post officers had to get the missiles up and running again immediately. To do so, though, they had to know what had gone wrong.

When the silos were checked, it was discovered that a fault in the guidance system of each missile had caused the malfunctions. Nobody had a clue why. The sites had not lost electric power per se, and the missiles showed no signs of tampering.

It *was* known that the only thing that could interfere with an ICBM's guidance system was an electromagnetic pulse—a big one—targeted directly at the missile's shielded circuits. While it was technically possible to produce such a huge power surge, it would require highly specialized equipment to do so. Such equipment did not exist at Malmstrom.

It took until late that night for maintenance crews to bring all the affected ICBMs back online. But there was no denying that on March 16, 1967, a significant part of America's nuclear arsenal would not have been available had an enemy chosen that day to attack the United States.

* * *

A week later, on March 24, an airman at one of Malmstrom's launch facilities spotted two bright objects in the sky.

They were moving in bizarre ways—so much so, the man called the base's deputy security officer. But for some unfathomable reason, especially in light of what had happened at the base just a week before, the security officer was unconvinced this was something important. He told the airman to alert him only if the objects came closer.

A minute later, the airman's terrified NCO (noncommissioned officer) called the security officer back and shouted that a red, saucer-shaped UFO was at that moment hovering outside the silo's gate.

After ordering the NCO to secure the site, the security officer contacted his commander. While the two men were discussing what to do, an alarm sounded throughout the command post. One of the base's missiles had gone offline. Ten seconds later, another missile went down. Then another and another.

In a virtual repeat of the events of the week before, in less than a minute, eight of Malmstrom's ICBMs had become inoperative.

One witness who'd helped restart this round of stricken missiles provided a personal account of what happened next, along with some baffling and unnerving details.

Before this man's particular replacement team left to begin their restart work, they received a special briefing from an NCO who told them starkly that the base was having big problems. UFOs were in the area, and they were shutting down the missile sites. The replacement crews were then given strict procedures on what to do if they saw a UFO out in the field.

The instructions went like this: If the crew saw a UFO

while approaching a missile silo, they should stop immediately and call in their location. If they should see a UFO after arriving at a silo, they should stop what they were doing and leave immediately. If they were actually working on a missile and saw a UFO, the team should take the missile's targeting tapes, then descend deep into the silo, closing all the hatches behind them.

This scenario would leave an unlucky guard behind, up on the surface. It would be his duty to report to the command post what was happening aboveground.

Luckily, none of these situations ever played out.

The Malmstrom commanders arranged for engineers from the Boeing Company, which had built the missiles, to examine their ICBMs and explain why they'd so mysteriously shut down. But the civilian contractors were baffled, too. One engineer who was there said no data could explain how or why the missiles were knocked off alert. However, neither the air force nor Boeing even considered UFOs in their analysis.

The cause of the Malmstrom shutdowns remains a mystery to this day.

"Launch in Progress!"—The Panic at Minot Air Force Base

Perhaps the most frightening UFO incursion at a U.S. ICBM facility happened at Minot Air Force Base three months after the bizarre events at Malmstrom.

Minot is located in the northern part of North Dakota.

In the 1960s, it was home to both an ICBM base and a wing of B-52 nuclear-armed bombers.

One night in late July 1967, base security personnel reported a large, bright object flying over the vast Minot range. Subsequent reports said the object was moving from missile silo to missile silo. Within an hour, *all* of Minot's launch facilities had reported that a UFO had been over their location.

Then suddenly, as the UFO passed over one particular site, the missile's indicators started flashing: "Launch in Progress."

Minot was no stranger to UFO incursions.

One night earlier that year, NORAD had contacted Minot's command post with an urgent message: A UFO was, at that moment, descending over one of Minot's missile silos. NORAD knew this because there were tracking the intruder on their all-powerful, all-seeing radars.

Minot's base command immediately dispatched a security team to investigate the situation. Arriving at the silo, the astonished security team saw a metallic disk-shaped object, surrounded with bright flashing lights, moving over their heads.

Suddenly the UFO stopped and went into a hover 500 feet above the missile silo. In the meantime, NORAD had scrambled two F-106s to intercept the UFO, but it disappeared before they arrived.

Now, on this hot July night, Minot's control room personnel were looking at a "Launch in Progress" warning. The control room personnel rushed to activate the missile's "Inhibit" switch. The procedure was successful, and eventually all of the missile's indicators returned to normal.

But it was apparent to all concerned that the UFO had probed the missile's controls and had somehow switched them on. Had any of the inhibit commands failed, the missile would have launched.

Still, the following day, one of the base's top officers announced to everyone involved that officially, "Nothing happened."

Interestingly, a comparable event occurred in the Soviet Union about fifteen years later. In October 1982, a saucer-shaped UFO appeared over an ICBM base near Byelokoroviche, a village in Ukraine. Many of the villagers, as well as base personnel, saw the object.

While the UFO hung over the base, the automated launch sequence on several missiles within was suddenly activated. A missile engineer at the base, interviewed in 1997 on ABC's *Primetime Live*, recounted how the launch crew watched helplessly as the countdown continued for fifteen terrifying seconds. Then, just as suddenly, the sequence aborted and the missiles returned to their normal standby status.

Another retired army officer who was there added: "During this period, for a short time, signal lights on both the control panels suddenly turned on. The lights showing the missiles were preparing for launch. This could normally only happen if an order were transmitted from Moscow."

Official explanations later said that the hovering object had been a "military flare."

An "Inspection" at Malmstrom

In 1966, the United States began a program to upgrade its long-range nuclear-armed missiles.

All of SAC's ICBMs were replaced with either the Minuteman II or the Minuteman III missiles, requiring a complete renovation of all of the air force's launch facilities. This immense task was finally completed in January 1975, but according to a report on NUFORC, UFO sightings still continued unabated at SAC's ICBM bases throughout this period.

For instance, in early January 1972, Malmstrom Air Force Base received an odd report from the nearby NORAD headquarters. Sensors around one of Malmstrom's missile silos showed that the ground temperature had inexplicably risen some 80 degrees Fahrenheit in just a few minutes.

The Malmstrom watch commander quickly checked the silo in question. None of the silo's perimeter sensors had indicated any intrusion. Nor were there signs that anything had "walked up" to the site.

A security team was rushed to the silo; when they arrived they saw something incredible. A UFO was sitting on the ground, and the cover to the missile silo had been removed. Apparently the UFO's "crew" had broken into the launch facility.

The security team was close enough that, even though no description was ever recorded, one member claimed he saw the UFO crew inside the silo, examining the missile's circuitry. On being discovered, the UFO occupants hurried back their craft. The UFO lifted off, shooting straight up at a speed estimated to be 50,000 miles an hour.

Afterward, the controller and the shaken security

team were told by base higher-ups that the incident "didn't happen."

The Loring Mystery

Around Halloween 1975, Loring Air Force Base in Maine suddenly became the center of attention of the UFO incursions.

Located in the far northeastern corner of the state, very close to the Canadian border, this usually frigid place was not an ICBM base. It was the home of the 42nd Strategic Bomb Wing—and in the 1970s, "strategic" meant "nuclear." The base stored the hydrogen weapons that U.S. B-52 bombers would drop on the Soviet Union in the event of war.

As documented extensively by NICAP, on the evening of October 27, 1975, a member of the base security police saw what he thought was an airplane, flying unusually low along the base's northern perimeter.

The unidentified craft had also appeared on the base radar. The control tower officer tried to contact the errant aircraft to warn it off but met with no success. The ATC officer immediately reported the situation to Loring's base command.

A few minutes later, the wing commander arrived on the scene and called a high-level security alert.

Meanwhile, the mysterious "aircraft" began circling the base's nuclear weapons storage area, at this point flying only 150 feet off the ground. This continued for more than a half hour, even as security vehicles poured into the area, scouring the weapons facility and the ground directly beneath the intruder's flight path.

The mystery craft eventually disappeared, only to briefly reappear on radar again, heading in the direction of New Brunswick, Canada.

Loring's base command took this incident very seriously.

They notified the air force chief of staff and SAC headquarters, among others. The message they sent was clear: "The (intruder) definitely penetrated the Loring Air Force Base's perimeter."

Loring command also reached out to civilian authorities, including the FAA and state and local police. They wanted help in identifying the mysterious craft. But no one had any idea what it was or where it came from.

Then, the following night, it happened again. At the same hour, 7:45 P.M., a UFO approached the base. Brightly lit and clearly showing up on radar, it crossed the base perimeter and started moving toward the weapons storage area again. Witnesses watching from a distance said the UFO moved in stops and starts. At some point, its lights went off and the witnesses lost sight of it. A few moments later, though, it reappeared again just 150 feet above the weapons storage area.

This time, however, some base personnel got a closer look at the mysterious craft. Several members of a B-52 ground crew saw the UFO while it was hovering at the end of the flight line.

The men commandeered a nearby truck and sped toward the object. Their pursuit took them into the weapons storage area, where they got within a few hundred feet of the UFO. They would later describe the object as being as long as four cars put together and looking like an orange and red stretched-out football. They saw no propellers, rotors or wings.

One of the men said that what he observed made him think of the desert. "You see waves of heat rising off the desert floor," he was quoted in an affidavit later on. "This is what I saw. There were these waves in front of the object and all the colors were blending together. The object was solid and we could not hear any noise coming from it."

By this time the men *could* hear the sirens of the base security teams rushing to the scene. Being in a restricted area, where they had no right to be, the men turned their truck around and hurried back to the flight line. The police ignored them, though. They had more important things to worry about: namely, the strange object over the weapons area. As soon as their searchlights raked the area, the UFO took off.

As on the previous night, radar tracked the UFO as it headed toward New Brunswick.

Again, the base higher-ups sent priority messages about the intrusion to higher commands. They also braced themselves for further incidents.

They were wise to do so. On Halloween night, a UFO was spotted four miles northwest of the base. Anticipating just such an event, a base helicopter was immediately launched to intercept the object but had no success. The object disappeared. Two hours later the base radar center detected another unidentified object moving slowly within the base perimeter. The helicopter took off again, but as before, the crew found nothing.

Now the Loring detachment of the OSI sent a message to

higher authority. The message described another "unidenti-fied 'helicopter'" sighted at low level over Loring AFB over the past two nights (October 31–November 1). It also re-ferred to the intruder as an "unknown entity."

What makes all this even stranger is that Loring wasn't the only SAC base being probed by UFOs during this time. On the night of October 30, personnel at Wurtsmith Air Force Base in Michigan spotted what *they* thought was a helicopter flying around their perimeter. The object, which seemed to have one white light shining downward and two red lights at the rear, did not maintain a consistent altitude. Instead it was seen bobbing up and down.

A few minutes later, Wurtsmith's security police re-ported a second unidentified "helicopter" inside the perim-eter. Like the UFO at Loring, this craft hovered low over the nuclear weapons storage area. Base radar confirmed that there were two objects flying over the base at low altitudes.

Further confirmation came from the crew of a KC-135 that was airborne at the time. They caught glimpses of the two UFOs, but their plane could never get close enough to distinguish any details.

The Malmstrom 1975 Sightings

Once again, Malmstrom Air Force Base in Montana was the site of an ominous UFO incursion.

On November 7, 1975, an alarm sounded across the base, indicating that security at one of the base's missile silos had been violated. The two officers inside the particular launch facility had no way of seeing what was happening above them. Following standard procedures, they requested a security team to investigate.

As this team approached the silo, they reported seeing an enormous orange disk hovering low over the area. By one description it was at least 300 feet across. On hearing this, the officers down in the launch facility ordered the security team to continue to the site—but the security men refused to get any closer to the terrifying object.

The air force scrambled two F-106 jet interceptors from nearby Great Falls, but the disk took off before they arrived, roaring to a height of some 75,000 feet and quickly disappearing.

The base immediately sent technicians to the silo in question to check out the missile. To their horror, they discovered that the targeting info stored in the warhead's guidance system had been changed. The technicians were ordered to remove the reentry vehicle, which contained multiple nuclear warheads, from the missile. These warheads were then painstakingly checked at the base. But nobody could understand how the targeting info had been altered.

In the end, the entire missile was replaced.

The Straight Edge of Space

One of the eeriest stories Hastings tells in *UFOs and Nukes* took place in January 1979. It begins with a technical team working inside an ICBM launch silo at Ellsworth Air Force Base.

The team was performing a targeting alignment procedure on the missile, which is a painstaking process. Suddenly the site guard, who was patrolling up on ground level, started banging on the ladder that led underground. He told the techs to come up top immediately.

The team chief and one of his techs climbed out of the silo into the cold South Dakota night and were instantly deafened by a loud, low-frequency hum, a noise with no evident source. The vibration was so powerful it was shaking the access hatch and a truck parked next to it.

The frightened guard informed them that the noise had started five minutes before and that he had already reported it to the base command post.

But then the guard, even more terrified, told the men to look up into the sky. What they saw was incomprehensible. Right above them everything was black—featureless black. Yet when they looked off in any other direction they could see the starry night sky. Something was hovering right above them.

One technician later described what he saw as "a straight-edge in space" blocking off the stars. But the three men could make out no details of the object over their heads. They opened the gate on the north side of the silo and walked out, trying to follow on the ground what seemed to be the "boundary" of whatever was floating above them. Strangely, as soon as they stepped outside the security gate, the ear-splitting hum stopped.

They decided to walk the outline of the object above them. Turning three right angles before getting get back to their starting point, they later estimated that the sides of the object were 80 to 100 feet long and that it was shaped like a parallelogram.

As soon as the trio reentered the site, the loud hum engulfed them again. At that point, the technicians decided to go back down into the silo. But suddenly, *everything* at the site lost power, from the lights above- and belowground to the truck engine. Most troubling, the guard's radio had gone dead.

The technicians climbed back down into the silo anyway. They did the best they could to get the lights working again but failed. Since they could accomplish nothing useful inside the pitch-black silo, they returned to ground level again, worried now that *they* would be blamed for the power outage.

Much to their relief, everything was now quiet up top—but they could still see the UFO above them, blotting out the sky. Then, suddenly, the power returned. The lights snapped on; the entire sky was visible again. The object had disappeared.

But then it was discovered that the guidance system for the silo's missile was inoperative. The men had immediately begun the procedures needed to restart it when they got an angry call from the command facility. Indeed, the higher-ups thought the techs had caused the power outage at the site. The technicians assured the control facility they were as much in the dark as everyone else about what was going on. They were working to restore the guidance system and would finish the interrupted alignment procedure.

Like so many of the other witnesses to unexplained phenomena, the technicians knew what happened to people who reported UFOs. So, they agreed they would say nothing about the strange object in the sky. On leaving the site, they told the guard to stay quiet about what happened, too.

When the techs returned to base, though, they heard that crews working at two other silos had exactly the same experience as they had. They'd spotted an object overhead, the lights died and their missiles went off alert status.

All of the base leadership seemed to be at the hangar when the technicians dropped off their gear. This was odd enough. But then each man was put in a room by himself and told to fill out a detailed report about what had happened. Sticking to their agreement, the two technicians said nothing about a UFO.

Members of another team *did* report the UFO, however, and they were ordered to sign a national security agreement, vowing never to discuss the event again.

Later on it was learned that the power failures that night had been widespread. As many as thirteen missiles had gone off alert status.

Again, this is just a small sampling of UFO incursion incidents at America's ICBM bases.

Reports tapered off with the 1970s, but not completely. In fact, a UFO incursion at a U.S. missile base was reported as recently as 2005.

Still, there are fewer ICBMs these days, due to various disarmament treaties between the United States and Russia. Perhaps that's why there are fewer UFO sightings at nuclear missile bases.

But that still leaves the question: Why were UFOs so interested in these places? What were they doing? Surveillance? Sabotage? Or were they sending some kind of message?

The foo fighters seemed curious about the ways we've come to kill each other; maybe this was just another form of that inquisitiveness. Or maybe this was someone's way of telling us what we should already know: that these kinds of weapons could quickly destroy all of human civilization.

Or maybe it was something else altogether.

The biggest mystery of all, though, is why the U.S. military, and mostly the U.S. Air Force, chose to treat these incidents so cavalierly and/or deceptively.

Dr. J. Allen Hynek, the late great scientist who first worked for the air force in debunking UFO cases only to become a believer in them himself, published an article in 1972 about one of the UFO incursion incidents.

He reported that after the episode was "investigated," the air force's official explanation was that all the witnesses—from airmen to the base in question's high-ranking officers—were seeing "stars."

Hynek then asked facetiously: Was the U.S. Air Force putting in charge of the nuclear arsenal people who were so stupid that they didn't know a "star" when they saw one? These same people who someday might be called on to launch this country's nuclear weapons?

As with the cascade of UFO incidents in the 1950s and during the Korean conflict, the air force's actions—or inactions—when it came to the UFO ICBM incursions of the 1960s and '70s, like the incursions themselves, simply defy explanation.

17

Vietnam

In many ways, America's involvement in the Vietnam War was an exercise in military mismanagement.

Fought as part of the larger Indochina War, which ran from 1950 to 1975, from America's point of view, the heaviest combat occurred between 1965 and 1969 when the United States had more than 500,000 troops in the country and many thousands more in ships offshore and in nearby countries supporting the effort.

Essentially a civil war that the United States entered to help the somewhat democratic South Vietnam against the totalitarian communist North, it was a disastrous conflict with no set battle lines, no clear-cut U.S. strategy, few conventional battles and no tangible way to measure success except by body counts.

The war saw more bombs dropped on relatively tiny North Vietnam than on the entirety of Europe during World War II. Hundreds of jet fighters and bombers took to the skies daily, unleashing everything from terrifying "daisy cutter" bombs, to napalm and cluster bombs, to advanced weaponry like the first "smart" bombs, to massive carpet-bombing raids performed by B-52s loaded with conventional weapons instead of nukes.

It also involved this huge, half-million-man U.S. ground force whose members were required to do duty in the war zone for just one year and then go home. For many of these troops, fully aware that what they were doing was universally unpopular, catastrophically destructive, with no chance for a clear-cut victory, the idea wasn't so much fight to win but more to just stay alive for those twelve months and then hopefully get out. Sadly, 58,000 of them didn't make it.

There was much heroism in Vietnam, and many brave American soldiers and marines died in what they considered service to their country. But by the admission of many, and by the historical record, there was much drug use and abuse during the Vietnam War as well. American troops went into combat stoned on marijuana or worse. Hallucinogenics were not uncommon in the fighting units or in the rear areas; heroin was readily available, too. At the height of the American involvement, one section of the South's capital city, Saigon, was considered such a dangerous drug haven for AWOL U.S. soldiers, even the military authorities refused to go there.

It is no surprise then that many of the reports of UFOs from this luckless war—happening at the same time as the frightening UFO ICBM incursions episode—are as chaotic as the war itself. Many sound more like science fiction than scientific mystery. And oddly, most come from ground forces and not from those flying through the air.

With thanks to UFO Casebook, Brian Vike's HBBC UFO Research, the Australian UFO Research Network's Jon Wyatt and others, what follows are a few of the most unusual—and infamous—UFO episodes of the Vietnam War.

UFO Kills Machinery

Maybe one of the strangest UFO incidents of *any* war took place in 1966 at the height of the Vietnam conflict. It happened at a place called Nha Trang, and if the reported accounts are correct, the sighting might have been witnessed by hundreds, or maybe thousands, of U.S. soldiers.

The incident was initially investigated by the original NICAP, the National Investigations Committee on Aerial Phenomena; this story comes from its archived files.

At the time of the reported episode, June 1966, Nha Trang was a massive joint U.S.-South Vietnamese military base and one of the most heavily defended installations in the country. Located along South Vietnam's central coastline, the base was actually situated in a valley, with highlands to the west and the South China Sea to the east.

The story of what happened went like this: According to the witness who originally reported the incident to NICAP, the base was abuzz with activity this particular night. A construction crew using more than a half dozen bulldozers was cutting roads around a hill about a half mile west of the base. Two Skyraider fighter-bombers were warming up on the base runway about a mile to the east, getting ready to take off. Meanwhile, a large group of U.S. soldiers were in an open area somewhere in between, all set to watch an outdoor movie. The recent addition of a small electrical generator had made such open-air entertainment possible.

According to the witness, the movie started around 8 P.M. and ran for a while without any problems. But around 9:45, the sky around the base suddenly turned extremely bright. At first the cause seemed to be a flare lit off over a hill to the north of the base. The troops at Nha Trang were used to seeing flares being fired around the base's defense perimeters, so initially no one in the crowd of moviegoers gave it much thought.

But then the light did not go away—and it was soon obvious this was not a flare illuminating the huge military installation. It was a luminous object hovering high above the base. Some fighter pilots in the crowd estimated the object was at least five miles up. But no one knew *what* it was.

Suddenly the object began dropping straight down, heading right for the base. But before a full-scale panic could break out, it stopped in midair. Now it was just 500 feet above the crowd, and at this point the witness said not just the base, but the entire valley around it was lit up like daytime. That's how bright the object was.

Then, just as suddenly, the object shot straight up and out of sight. It was gone in seconds, returning the valley to darkness again and leaving the hundreds of soldiers dumbstruck.

But the strangeness didn't end there. According to the witness, as soon as the luminous object appeared, the bulldozers clearing the road, the two Skyraider airplanes warming up and even the generator that was providing power to run the movie projector all suddenly stopped working.

The witness said: "There wasn't a car, truck, plane or anything running for about four minutes."

Again according to the witness, the next day a plane carrying investigators from the United States arrived at Nha Trang. Presumably, they spoke to some of those involved and examined the affected machinery.

But what conclusions they came to, if any, remain unknown.

Giant Saves GI

During the long years of war, a stretch of no-man's-land split Vietnam in two, almost evenly, north from south. Approximately a mile wide, and more than 50 miles long, it was called the Demilitarized Zone, but was more commonly known as the DMZ.

One afternoon, in late 1966, the witness in this odd incident was part of a U.S. Army helicopter force touching down in a landing zone close to the DMZ.

The communist enemy had opened up on the helicopters as they were landing. The American soldiers in the helicopters returned fire, and a full-scale battle was soon in progress.

Because the landing zone was covered with waist-high dry grass, several grass fires erupted as a result of the gunfire going back and forth.

Suddenly one of the helicopters ran into a problem. Experiencing engine trouble once on the ground, it now had both the enemy and grass fires surrounding it.

The commanding officer of the landing force told the witness to grab a fire extinguisher from his helicopter and run back to the stricken one, hopefully to help rescue its crew.

The soldier did as ordered, taking the fire extinguisher but leaving his weapon behind. But upon getting close to the damaged copter, he saw its crew waving him away—the engine problem had been fixed and the helicopter was taking off.

The soldier turned to return to his helicopter—but the smoke and flames from the grass fires, plus the firefight still going on around him, had him disoriented. In seconds, he was hopelessly lost.

Suddenly he heard someone yelling in Vietnamese. He turned to see an enemy soldier pointing his weapon at him. The American trooper, being unarmed, was sure his end was near.

Then he heard a loud *crack*! He was certain he'd been shot but weirdly felt no pain. Instead he turned to see the enemy soldier fall to the ground, dead. That's when the U.S. soldier looked up and saw an astonishing sight.

A figure at least eight feet tall was standing nearby. This creature was dressed "perfectly," in the witness's words, with a sort of helmet covering most of his face. There was an aura around it—and somehow this giant had killed the enemy soldier and saved the American's life.

This creature was not of this earth; this much seems clear. Yet it spoke to the American soldier, telling him all was okay and that he should return to his helicopter.

The soldier did as told and ran back to his copter unharmed.

As the helicopter took off, the man could see the dead enemy soldier, but there was no sign of the giant who'd saved his life.

"Charlie" Fires at UFO

Located on the south central coast of Vietnam, Da Nang was a huge American base utilized by all four of the U.S. services: Army, Air Force, Navy and Marines. The vast installation was a seaport, boasted thousands of ground troops and was home to a massive air base.

Close to Da Nang was a location called Red Beach. The First U.S. Marine Division had a supply base there. There was a very dangerous place nearby, an enemy-infested area known as the A Shau Valley. One entrance to this valley was close to the First Division's supply base, and at night marines would sneak into the darkened jungle and set up ambushes, hoping to catch enemy forces by surprise. The marines called it "Hunting Charlie."

One night in March 1967, a small group of marines left Red Beach and slipped into the valley. They walked two miles in and established their ambush site near a trail the enemy was known to frequent.

But the enemy chose not to walk down this particular trail that night, so there was no ambush, no combat. By morning, the marines were headed back to camp.

It was on this return trip that the strangeness began. The marines were passing through an open area when suddenly there was a huge object above them. The object could be seen clearly hovering just over the top of the jungle canopy.

The marines stared at it in astonishment, but they did not open fire on it. However, there were enemy troops nearby, and they started shooting at the object with everything they had. This included rocket-propelled grenades and a fusillade of machine-gun fire.

Yet in shades of the Loreto incident in Italy in World War II, nothing shot at the object seemed to have any effect on it.

The enemy eventually stopped firing at the UFO. Moments later, it accelerated quickly and disappeared at a high rate of speed. In all, the marines had it in sight for at least five minutes.

The marines finally resumed their march back to Red Beach. Later on, their commanding officer told them never to mention the incident to anybody.

UFOs Chasing Phantoms

Da Nang, again. 1968. Early morning. Four marines were sitting at the end of the air base's runway.

They were watching two F-4 Phantom jets getting ready to take off. The F-4 was accurately described back then as a flying dump truck. A massive two-engine fighter-bomber, it could carry almost two and a half times the bomb load of a B-17 Flying Fortress—this while flying twice the speed of sound. The marines watched the pair of F-4s take off and climb into the sky—but then they spotted two strange lights flying over the base as well. Incredibly, those lights began following the Phantoms—and then, a few seconds later, they were joined by six *more* lights.

At first the marines thought the lights were North Vietnamese MiGs—as unlikely as that would be, because the communist air force never ventured below the DMZ. But on calling the base ATC tower, the marines were told there were no "unknown" blips on the radar screen. In other words, the F-4s were being chased by eight UFOs.

The marines continued watching the unfolding drama and saw the F-4s, apparently aware of their situation, quickly alter their flight plans and turn back for the base. Yet the lights were still following them; in fact, they stayed with the Phantoms almost right down to the runway itself. At this point the marines were astonished to see that the lights were actually oval-shaped objects with multiple beams emanating from them. Each beam was giving off an amber glow.

The objects finally stopped following the F-4s a few hundred feet before they landed. The marines watched as the objects hovered there for a while before turning skyward and leaving the area at high speed.

The UFO and the Hit Squad

During much of the Vietnam War, the U.S. military, sometimes in conjunction with the CIA, ran special operations throughout Indochina.

The goal of many of these top secret missions was to hunt down high-ranking communist officials and political figures and, in CIA-speak, "terminate them with extreme prejudice." Translation: Assassinate them.

In other words, these special ops units were hit squads.

During August 1968, one of these teams infiltrated North Vietnam, found their target and assassinated him. But on starting their withdrawal, they were detected by the enemy and a chase ensued.

The team had to get back to their pickup point, the predetermined location where they would meet a helicopter to extract them from North Vietnam.

Getting close to this point by midmorning, with the enemy

still on their tails, the team found themselves in front of two hills. They climbed the one to their left, hoping this choice would help them avoid capture.

Just as the team was getting under cover, they heard the unmistakable chattering sound of AK-47 assault rifles firing from the next hill over. Enemy soldiers were nearby. But what were they shooting at?

The hit squad saw the enemy tracers going nearly straight up into the sky. The assassins were certain they were firing at their extraction aircraft—but they were in for a surprise.

Instead of seeing their rescue copter, they saw a large semicircular object appear over the hill next to their position. It was immediately clear this was not an aircraft that belonged to either side. This was a UFO, strange and alien. One member of the team recalled that its color kept changing from light blue to bright red. It was making no noise.

As soon as the enemy tracers got close to the object, it suddenly stopped in midair, just a few hundred feet from where the U.S. special ops team was hiding.

The Americans saw a streak of light shoot out from the front of the object—then there was nothing but silence. The enemy barrage had ceased.

The UFO briefly lingered over the spot where the enemy had been firing at it, then turned and headed out to sea.

The hit squad waited about thirty minutes. Hearing no more enemy activity, they descended their hill and went to look around the enemy position. What they found was as startling as seeing the UFO itself. There were no enemy bodies, according to one member of the special ops team. Just the enemy's weapons—and they'd been melted down to almost nothing, leaving a smell that was so bad, it stayed with the team members for hours afterward.

The team's copter finally arrived and lifted them out. On returning to their base, one of the members immediately reported the incident to the higher-ups. The other team members never saw him again.

Those remaining didn't say anything about the incident during their postmission debriefings. But soon after, they were questioned directly about it, not by military brass, but by civilians.

Their method of interrogation was extremely unusual. According to one team member, the civilians blindfolded each remaining member of the hit squad, taping their mouths shut as well. They were brought, individually, to an undisclosed location and put in a small room. Inside the room were three men; one wore a hood, keeping his face hidden. This person remained silent the whole time. According to one team member, when the questioning was over, all he recalled was seeing a bright flash of light. The next thing he knew he was back at his base, as were the others in his team.

Startled, he tried to talk to his colleagues about what had just happened, but none of them had any memory of the interrogation or the encounter with the UFO that preceded it. Only he did.

Thinking that to mention it again might be dangerous, the team member decided to keep the story to himself.

Years went by. The team member got married, eventually left the army and moved to Alaska.

One day, he and his wife were in their boat fishing when suddenly a UFO was hovering right above them. Completely astonished, the team member realized it was the *exact same* UFO he'd seen years before in Vietnam.

The UFO remained hovering over the boat for a few moments and then disappeared—this time, for good.

Batwoman Spotted

Once again, near Da Nang in the summer of 1969, a soldier was pulling guard duty.

Suddenly, he saw something coming out of the night, flying toward him. It was not an aircraft or a bird. Rather, it was a naked woman, her skin all black, with huge bat wings. Her body was glowing brightly.

The soldier had the batwoman in sight for almost four minutes before she finally flew away.

UFO Over Hanoi

On September 29, 1972, the Agence France-Presse (AFP) news organization reported that a UFO had appeared over the North Vietnamese capital city of Hanoi.

The AFP's Hanoi correspondent filed the following lead: "A mysterious object appeared in the clear blue sky over Hanoi Friday, attracting missile fire from the ground but apparently remaining motionless."

The reporter saw the object himself through binoculars. His description was as follows: "It was spherical in shape and a luminous orange in color, and was clearly at a very high altitude . . . North Vietnamese air defenses fired three surface-to-air missiles, [but they] were unable to reach the target . . . The object remained in the same high spot for over one hour and 20 minutes, although towards the end it appeared less bright than before."

Close to the DMZ

Date unknown. Late one night, almost midnight, two marines on watch near their base perimeter heard a strange sound. In one man's description, it was like the wind rustling way off in the distance.

The sound got closer over the next five minutes. Finally, it became so intense, it started rattling the cans tied to the camp's barbed wire.

Then the marines saw it right above them. It was a disk, all black, no more than 200 feet off the ground. And it was huge.

So huge, it took almost a minute for it to pass completely overhead.

The marines later reported that though they were in a free-fire zone, no one shot at the UFO.

The *Hobart* Incident

One UFO episode stands out in the Vietnam War.

This one did not involve disillusioned grunts seeing strange things in the sky, or compassionate giants, or anticommunist flying saucers.

This incident was extensively reported by Jon Wyatt of the Australian UFO Research Network and others. It involves a night of confusion, mistaken identity, a high-speed aerial chase and, in the end, a deadly tragedy. And as with a lot of UFO incidents, it left more questions than answers.

It started on the night of June 15, 1968. U.S. military observers stationed along the eastern part of the DMZ saw strange lights moving slowly across the sky.

What could these lights be? The observers theorized the "lights" were North Vietnamese helicopters carrying troops and supplies across the DMZ. Suspecting a new enemy offensive might be building, the U.S. military did three things: They rushed large numbers of antiaircraft weapons up to the DMZ, they put U.S. Air Force fighters at Da Nang air base on high alert and they asked that all available allied warships in the area be assigned to patrol off the DMZ's coast.

The Australian Navy destroyer HMAS *Hobart* was one of those warships.

It should be noted the North Vietnamese did not use helicopters during the Vietnam War, at least not after 1965. And even if they had, the communists would have been foolish to fly them over the DMZ and into South Vietnam's airspace, as they would have been quickly shot down by American forces. Yet, the U.S. military could not come up with any other explanation for the objects spotted flying over the DMZ.

The mysterious lights reappeared the following night, once again detected moving along the eastern edge of the DMZ. Several U.S. Air Force fighter planes were dispatched to the scene, intent on engaging the intruders. U.S. antiaircraft guns also fired at the unknown aircraft. That's when the lights were seen moving off the coast and out to the sea.

Disaster soon followed.

At about 3:30 A.M., the HMAS *Hobart* was in position off the coast of the DMZ when its crew detected an aircraft approaching. The ship was attempting to contact the aircraft when a missile slammed into its starboard side, killing one sailor and injuring two others. Seconds later, two more missiles hit the *Hobart*, killing another sailor and injuring several more. The *Hobart*'s gun crews fired on the attacker but scored no hits.

An investigation later determined the missiles came from U.S. fighter planes whose pilots thought they were firing at the mysterious lights. The missiles missed their intended targets and hit the Australian destroyer instead. The next morning, American helicopters airlifted the injured sailors off the *Hobart*, and the heavily damaged destroyer headed to Subic Bay in the Philippines for repairs.

What was it that appeared over the DMZ that led to the *Hobart* being attacked? Wyatt points out that Australian history books mention unusual atmospheric conditions over the DMZ the night of the tragedy—but this seems an unlikely cause. Whatever the "lights" were, they were sighted many times after the *Hobart* incident. The Melbourne *Sun* said: "[Subsequent] sightings were reported by radar men in Quang Tri Province about five miles below the DMZ. It was the sixth time since [the *Hobart* was hit] that such sightings have been reported. U.S. command ordered its fighters and artillery to withhold fire not wanting a repeat of the incidents in which the Allied ships were fired upon."

Adding to the mystery, no evidence of any enemy helicopters was ever found—no wreckage or landing sites. Plus, no large offensive linked to the "helicopters" ever materialized. In August 1968, the *Royal Australian Navy News* confirmed: "Extensive reconnaissance produced no evidence of enemy helicopter operations in or near the DMZ."

The late General George S. Brown was commander of

the U.S. Seventh Air Force at the time of the incident; he was in charge of the jet fighters involved in the *Hobart* attack.

Years later, Brown became chairman of the Joint Chiefs of Staff, the highest position in the U.S. military. As reported by John Wyatt, in 1973, Brown was quoted as saying: "UFOs plagued us in Vietnam. They weren't called UFOs, they were called 'enemy helicopters.' They were only seen at night and only in certain places. They were seen up around the DMZ in the early summer of 1968, and this resulted in quite a battle. And in the course of this, an Australian destroyer took a hit. There was no enemy at all involved, but we always reacted. Always after dark."

George Filer, who later became a UFO researcher, served as an air force intelligence officer under General Brown during the Vietnam conflict. He was also reported by Wyatt as saying: "In 1968, I briefed General Brown most mornings on the intelligence situation in Vietnam. A lot of times we'd get UFO reports over the DMZ."

The origin of the mysterious lights was never determined.

PART SEVEN

Other Sightings

18

Three Enduring Mysteries

Kecksburg

While the Vietnam War raged with the whole world watching and bizarre UFO incursions were secretly plaguing America's ICBM bases, other UFO incidents were occurring, including several of a highly unusual nature involving the U.S. military.

One is known as the Kecksburg incident. It has remained one of the most enduring UFO mysteries to date, perhaps because so many people believe that unlike Roswell, in this case, the U.S. military *did* indeed retrieve an intact UFO—or something that looked a lot like one.

It all started on December 5, 1965, a cold late autumn afternoon across the upper portion of the United States. People in Canada, Michigan and Ohio saw something strange flying through their skies. Described as bright and fiery, it caused sonic booms over Detroit and was spotted by pilots over Lake Erie.

Many eyewitnesses thought it was a meteorite, but others would say later that the object seemed to be under intelligent control, moving as if it was being steered and apparently turning at a sharp angle over eastern Ohio before finally crashing to earth. By most reports, whatever it was came to rest in western Pennsylvania about 40 miles southeast of Pittsburgh near a small town named Kecksburg.

Several Kecksburg citizens saw something fall into a heavily wooded area around 6:30 P.M. These witnesses claimed that instead of coming in at full speed as a meteorite or a piece of space debris would, the object more or less glided in, avoiding some obstacles before finally coming down in the woods. A column of blue smoke was seen rising over the trees shortly afterward.

The local radio station was called, and they in turn contacted the Pennsylvania State Police. A volunteer fire unit went into the woods along with the local fire marshal and some state troopers. Meanwhile, anxious residents waited nearby wondering what they would find.

When the fire marshal finally emerged, he ordered the woods sealed off and indicated to witnesses that "the army" would soon be holding a news conference on the matter. But a short time later, the state police made a contradictory announcement: They'd found nothing in the woods. Nothing at all. This left residents more confused than ever.

But then, a third player came on the scene: the U.S. military.

According to many witnesses, military personnel—both army and air force—flooded into the small town, sealing off the woods and taking over the fire hall and other buildings. Soon afterward, a flatbed truck was brought in, only to be seen later on leaving town, carrying something covered by a tarpaulin.

Despite all this intrigue, many people believed the original statement from the state police that nothing unusual had been found in the woods.

And this was pretty much how the incident stayed—until twenty-five years later, when a national TV show did an episode on the Kecksburg mystery.

It was revealed on this broadcast that before the police and the military secured the woods, several civilians had made their way to the crash site and got a glimpse at what had come down there. Though their accounts varied a bit, for the most part, they came up with a fairly cohesive description: The object was actually some kind of capsule, shaped somewhere between a saucer and a huge acorn and at least 12 feet in length. It had a gold band around its middle and was copper in color. There were also claims that hieroglyphic-style writing was seen on the object.

No surprise then that the incident has been called "Pennsylvania's Roswell." But even after the show's revelations, further inquiries to the military went nowhere.

The story had another troubling aspect. John Murphy was a local radio reporter for the Kecksburg area. He was on the scene of the incident even before the police were, and way before the military arrived. He'd supposedly taken photographs of the object in the woods. He was also there when the fire marshal cleared the woods and when the state police announced nothing had been found. Like many townspeople, Murphy wondered if nothing had been found, then why had the woods been cordoned off? And why had the small army of military people descended on tiny Kecksburg?

Murphy prepared a special radio documentary on the incident, titled *Object in the Woods*. But just before he was going to broadcast the report, Murphy was visited by two mysterious men in black, an event corroborated by other radio station employees. Murphy was taken to a back room at the radio station and questioned. When he emerged thirty minutes later, he appeared shaken. Plus, his photographs of the crash site had been confiscated. Later on, when Murphy finally aired his report, it had been so heavily censored, the "object in the woods" of the title wasn't even mentioned.

Murphy was said to have become extremely despondent after this. Apparently whatever the men in black told him had disillusioned him to the point that he refused to talk about the incident to anyone.

Years later, while visiting Ventura, California, Murphy was killed in a hit-and-run accident as he was crossing the street.

The driver was never caught.

There was an alternate explanation for the Kecksburg incident. The day it happened, December 5, 1965, a Russian space capsule called Cosmos 96 had come crashing to earth. This Russian probe was undeniably acorn shaped and roughly fit the description townspeople had given for the mystery object in the woods. However, at the time, both U.S. and Russian officials insisted the Cosmos probe had fallen to earth earlier that day, a full thirteen hours before the hubbub in Kecksburg. What's more, they said it had crashed in eastern Canada and not anywhere inside the United States. Still, it seemed like an odd coincidence.

Then in 2005, NASA came clean, sort of. One space agency official admitted that he had indeed studied fragments of the debris found in the Kecksburg woods and that they had come from a Soviet satellite. But in practically the same breath, the official said that the rest of the information NASA had relating to the incident had been "misplaced." A further twist occurred in 2007 when the same NASA official revealed that he'd been "inaccurate" when speaking about the incident and the evidence two years before, which seemed to put everything back to square one.

UFO researcher Stan Gordon probably knows more about the Kecksburg incident than anyone else in the field—and he has no plans on giving up. "I am still continuing my investigation," he told us in an interview. "New details have come to my attention and in recent years some additional witnesses have been located . . . I remain hopeful that someday we will find definitive proof of what was recovered in those Pennsylvania woods so long ago."

Today, a large re-creation of an acorn-shaped object covered with indecipherable hieroglyphics sits on a platform across the street from the Kecksburg fire station, a reminder of the small town's still-unsolved mystery.

The Coyne Incident

If there can be such a thing as a leisurely helicopter ride, that was the case on the night of October 18, 1973.

The helicopter was a UH-1, the ubiquitous Huey. This particular copter belonged to the U.S. Army Reserve base at Cleveland Hopkins International Airport, in Cleveland, Ohio.

Its crew was made up of civilian soldiers. Lieutenant Ar-rigo Jezzi was one of the pilots. Sergeant John Healey and Sergeant Robert Yanacsek were riding in back. The flight commander was the other pilot, Captain Lawrence Coyne.

The crew was making the short flight from Port Colum-bus, Ohio, to Cleveland, about a 100-mile trip. The weather was clear; the night was filled with stars. Perfect conditions for flying.

A leisurely flight. So relaxed, Coyne was smoking a cig-arette.

But then around 10:30 P.M., Sergeant Healey saw a red light off in the distance—and that's when the flight became distinctly *un*-leisurely.

The copter was flying at 100 miles per hour and about 3,000 feet in altitude when Healey first noticed the red light. All aircraft are equipped with navigation lights, and for fixed-wing aircraft, there is always a red light on the left-side wing.

So when Healey spotted the red light off to the west, he thought it was just another aircraft and didn't mention it to the others. A short while later, though, Yanacsek also saw the red light on the horizon and, after watching it for a short while, finally mentioned it to Coyne. The commander calmly sug-gested he just keep an eye on it.

But then Yanacsek saw the light turn toward the Huey and start to grow rapidly in size. In seconds, the light was heading for a collision with the helicopter.

Yanacsek called out in alarm, and Coyne acted instantly. Taking the controls from Jezzi, he put the Huey into a gut-wrenching dive, at the same time somehow calling nearby Mansfield airfield on the radio. Coyne was convinced one of Mansfield's Air National Guard jet fighters was coming at him. But just as Coyne heard the first words of reply from the Mansfield ATC tower, the Huey's radio went dead. And still the red light was coming right at them, even as the Huey continued to dive.

The crew braced for a collision. The red light was right on them.

But then, suddenly, it just . . . stopped.

When the astonished crew finally opened their eyes, they saw a gray cigar-shaped craft right in front of them, flying in unison with the Huey. The craft was enormous.

The red light the copter crewmen had first spotted was on the craft's bow. A white light was on its stern, and it had a green light underneath. A beam from this green light momentarily enveloped the copter's cockpit before shutting off.

The giant craft continued pacing them for about ten seconds. Then it took off at blinding speed, first heading west, then executing a sharp turn north before it finally blinked out.

Somehow Coyne regained control of the copter and his faculties and was able to fly to a safe landing in Cleveland.

As UFO sightings go, this one was very dramatic. But what makes it even more interesting was that there were ground witnesses as well.

As reported by nuforc.com, follow-up research by ufologists located a woman and four youths who'd been driving in the area at the time of the incident. They reported seeing a bright red light flying over their heads at one point, but then they lost sight of it.

The group continued driving and soon after saw two bright lights, these being red and green. The driver pulled to the side of the road, and incredibly, the car's occupants witnessed the exact moment that the UFO had stopped in front of the Huey helicopter and then begun flying along with it. The five witnesses even reported seeing the green ray of light envelop the helicopter before the UFO sped off.

Many ufologists call the "Coyne Incident" one of the best UFO sightings ever.

And though it was never explained, the copter crew won $5,000 from the *National Enquirer* for the most "scientifically valuable" report of 1973.

The Rendlesham Affair

It was the East Anglia section of Great Britain that was first haunted by the scareships of 1909.

Above its fields and villages, its cliffs and rugged coastline, the phantom blimps sailed through the night, pointing their mysterious searchlights down at everything and nothing, puzzling and frightening the population and giving the world its first peek at the men in black.

Flash forward forty-eight years, to the night of May 20, 1957—and once again something very strange is happening over East Anglia.

That night, two U.S. Air Force F-86 fighter jets stationed at the RAF base at Manston were scrambled to intercept an unknown flying object that had suddenly appeared over East Anglia. The object had not only bypassed the network of radar stations ringing the UK, it was also seen performing some very unearthly aerial maneuvers, such as flying extremely fast, then suddenly coming to a complete stop, before flying extremely fast again.

Even though this was happening during the Cold War, those bizarre flight characteristics guaranteed this was not a Soviet aircraft probing the British defenses.

This was a UFO.

The scramble flight was led by U.S. Air Force lieutenant Milton Torres. The Sabres had just reached the prescribed altitude of 32,000 feet when Torres received an order he did not expect: The UFO had been judged a security threat, so ground control told him to prepare his weapons to fire at it.

Torres's F-86 carried both machine guns and rockets, designed to stop incoming Soviet bombers. But now they were going to be used against something from out of this world—literally.

Torres looked down at his radar screen and saw the blip of the UFO. It was glowing extremely bright, meaning the target was enormous.

Within a few seconds, Torres had been able to get in behind the UFO. He armed his weapons and was about to fire when the object suddenly accelerated to tremendous speed. In an instant, it was off the Sabre's radar screen completely.

Torres later estimated the UFO must have attained at least Mach 10—as in 6,500 miles per hour—in order to make such a quick exit. However fast it went, though, it left the pair of Sabres flying through an empty sky.

(Oddly, a similar incident had happened just a year before, again over East Anglia; this one involved another huge UFO and as many as four jet fighters in pursuit ready to fire. Like the one Torres was chasing, that UFO also accelerated to an astonishing velocity just before its pursuers could unleash their weapons.)

Torres and his wingman landed back at Manston soon after their encounter, only to find that Torres was about to have a Man in Black episode of his own. A man Torres described as looking like a "well-dressed salesman" came to RAF Manston to interrogate him.

This man asked many questions about Torres's just completed mission. Once he'd got all the facts, the man informed Torres that the whole affair was now considered highly classified and that Torres should not talk about it with anybody, including his superior officers.

The mystery man also made it clear that if Torres said a word to anyone, his air force career would be terminated.

Flash forward another twenty-three years, to 1980—and *again*, strange doings in East Anglia.

This time it was in a place called Rendlesham Forest, a vast six-square-mile woodland near the city of Ipswich. The forest shared some interesting real estate. Located close to the coast, a nearby island housed some buildings purportedly occupied by the National Security Agency, America's most secretive intelligence agency. Also close by was a pair of large NATO air bases, RAF Woodbridge and RAF Bentwaters.

These bases were highly classified installations in 1980. RAF Bentwaters was one of NATO's largest nuclear weapon storage facilities at the time, and RAF Woodbridge was where the USAF 67th Aerospace Rescue and Recovery Squadron called home. This highly specialized unit was under the direct command of the Department of Defense and flew radically adapted HC-130 aircraft used for satellite recovery.

On the night of December 26, 1980, a blip appeared on

radar screens at RAF Watton in nearby Norfolk. This blip fell off the radar right in the area of Rendlesham Forest. The same unidentified object was also spotted by radar at RAF Bentwaters—and its track also ended over Rendlesham. Two U.S. Air Force policemen, John Burroughs and Budd Parker, were manning the east gate at RAF Woodbridge at the time. Around 2 A.M., they saw an object fall into the forest nearby. They thought it was one of the base's planes crashing, despite the fact that it was the Christmas holiday and no planes were supposed to be flying that night.

Then they saw lights coming from the dense forest. Not flames—instead they described them as looking like bulbs on a Christmas tree: A large yellow light was glowing above the trees, a red blinking light was in the center, and near it, a steady blue light. The lights were about a mile and a half east of the east gate.

What the policemen were looking at didn't make sense. First, they'd thought something had crashed in the woods— but now it was as if something had *landed* there. But how could something land safely in a thick forest?

The policemen called the base headquarters, and their sergeant was quickly on the scene. His name was Jim Penniston.

Penniston saw the lights in the forest as well and listened when his men insisted this was not a crashed plane. Whatever it was, Penniston knew it had to be investigated.

So, while Parker stayed at the gate, Sergeant Penniston, Burroughs and Penniston's driver set out for the woods.

But almost immediately the small search team's radios went on the blink. Something in the woods seemed to be interfering with them. Penniston ordered his driver to stay behind near the road, so he could shout messages to him if need be. Then Penniston and Burroughs went into the woods alone.

They noticed right away that strange things were happening. The forest animals were running around wildly, and the air seemed filled with electricity. They could feel the static on their skin. They heard strange noises, too. Burroughs reported hearing something like a woman screaming. Some farm animals nearby were making a lot of noise as well.

The two men started walking toward the lights, knowing if it was a downed aircraft, it would have lit the forest on fire by now or at the least filled the woods with the stink of spilled aviation fuel. Yet they could neither see nor smell anything along those lines. So Penniston and Burroughs stayed focused on the multiple colored lights, which were getting brighter as they approached.

They eventually reached a clearing, where they found the source of the strange illumination. It was a shiny object, shaped like a cone about five to six feet high. It was floating a couple of feet off the ground with a strange mist around it. It was so brightly colored that it was hard for the two men to make out any distinct features beyond that. But one thing was for certain: They were sure this was not something of this world.

Penniston eventually walked right up to the object. There appeared to be some strange writing etched on the side of it, but when he ran his hand over these impressions, the light on the top of the object suddenly grew brighter. Both men hit the dirt, and the object started moving away from them.

They watched as it made its way through the dense forest, finally reaching a spot a short distance away. At this point, the object ascended to about 200 feet above the ground, paused a moment, then took off at such high speed, both men said it was gone literally in the blink of an eye.

Thus began the haunting of Rendlesham Forest—and a real rarity: an almost indisputable UFO case.

And it was not over.

Penniston and Burroughs returned to the woods the next morning to find the local police on hand. The nearby constabulary had also received reports about the strange lights the night before, and they were investigating. At some point, the two airmen discovered indentations in the clearing where they believed the object had set down. Penniston and Burroughs measured the distance between these ground markings and found that they formed a perfect triangle, made, they were sure, by the undercarriage of the strange object. But the police did not agree with their conclusion. They insisted on describing these holes as animal diggings simply because they didn't want to put anything too crazy into their report.

But other signs of the UFO's presence were found as well. Many trees in the area had their tops broken off, and weird serrations were found on some tree trunks, too. Plus, a U.S. Air Force aircraft had flown over the area at sunrise and reported that infrared radiation was "pouring" out of the forest.

The base's top brass was made aware of all this, but typically, the U.S. Air Force refused to address the events.

Their stance was that whatever happened had taken place outside the gates of the Woodbridge base. Therefore, it was not their place to comment.

The following night there was an officers' dinner party at RAF Bentwaters.

No sooner had dinner begun, though, than a junior officer appeared and reported to the base commander that the UFO had returned to nearby Rendlesham Forest. Because the base commander was scheduled to make an after-dinner speech, he asked his deputy commander to handle it. This man was Lieutenant Colonel Charles Halt.

Halt gathered up some airmen and headed for the east gate. On arrival, Halt learned that an hour earlier a security patrol had spotted more strange lights floating above Rendlesham Forest. But the lights had quickly disappeared.

Still, Halt planned to go into the woods, fully intent on debunking all talk of a UFO. By his own words, he was convinced whatever was happening in Rendlesham had a rational explanation.

In addition to radios, Halt and his men had gas-powered lanterns called "light-alls" with them. Halt had also brought a small tape recorder with which he planned to record his thoughts and actions during the search.

He went into the forest with his men shortly after 1 A.M. The woods had been sealed off by this time; a security perimeter had been established so any curious locals or airmen wouldn't interfere with Halt's mission.

Once inside the forest, nothing seemed out of the ordinary, at least at first. But then the light-alls started cutting out, and soon after, the search party's radios began working only intermittently.

Then around 1:48 A.M., everything changed.

At that point on Halt's tape, the officer can be heard insisting his men slow down and take it easy. Why? Because they'd spotted the mysterious lights again.

At first, to Halt's eyes it looked like a glowing light resting on a pillar of yellowish mist. One of his men added that the light had a rainbow effect as well, as if being reflected through a prism. Just like the night before, the light was gliding slowly through the woods.

In interviews later on, Halt said he initially considered that the light might be an optical illusion, or a mirage, or that old standby, the weather-induced temperature inversion. But none of these explanations fit. On the tape he describes what he was looking at as being like a huge eye, with a dark center, winking at them. Halt also said the object appeared to have molten metal dripping off it, even though neither he nor his men could see any evidence of this on the ground.

Finally, Halt had to admit that he simply couldn't believe what he was seeing.

As reported on UFO researcher Nick Pope's website, nickpope.com, Halt was quoted as saying: "Here I am, a senior official that routinely denies this sort of thing, someone who diligently works to debunk them and [suddenly] I'm involved in the middle of something I can't explain."

The recording Halt made that night is as gripping as it is authentic. Spoken as a running commentary on his actions and those of his team, it is the sound of a man who had been a UFO skeptic minutes before becoming a UFO believer in a hurry.

(Note: The recording and transcript can be found on many Internet sites, including: www.ufos-aliens.co.uk/cosmicrend.html)

Halt: It's 0148, we're hearing very strange noises out of the farmer's barnyard animals. They're very, very active, making awful lot of noise . . . (pause) You just saw a light? Where?

Airman: Yeah . . .

Halt: Wait a minute now, slow down, where?

Airman: Right up in this position here, straight ahead, in between the tree . . . there it is again! Watch. Straight ahead . . . sir. There it is . . .

Halt: Yeah, I see it too. What is it?

Airman: We don't know, sir.

Halt: Yeah, it's a strange small red light, looks to be maybe a quarter to a half mile, maybe further out . . .

Halt: The light is gone now, it was approximately 120 degrees. Is it back again?

Airman: Yes sir.

Halt: Well, douse the flashlights then . . . let's go out to the edge of the clearing so I can get a better look at it . . . the light's still there and all the barnyard animals have gotten quiet now . . .

Airman: Now it's stopped. Now it's coming up, hold on, there we go. About four foot off the ground . . .

Halt: . . . Say that again. About four feet off the ground, about 110 degrees . . .

Airman: Yes sir. Now it's died.

Halt: . . . I think it's something that, something very weird.

Airman: How about the tree right over . . .

Halt: . . . The woods are just deadly calm. There is no

doubt about it, there's some type of strange flashing red light ahead.

Airman: There, it's yellow.

Halt: I saw a yellow tinge in it too. Weird, it, it appears that he may be moving this way? It's brighter than it has been.

Airman: Yellow . . .

Halt: It's coming this way! It's definitely coming this way! Pieces of it are shooting off. There is no doubt about it, this is . . . *weird.*

Airman: Two lights, one light to the right, one light to the left!

Halt: O.K., keep the flashlights off. There's something very, very strange . . . pieces are falling off it again.

Airman: And it just moved to the right.

Halt: Yeah!

Airman: Just off to the right.

Halt: O.K., we're looking at the thing, we're probably about . . . 300 yards away and it looks like an eye winking at you. It's still moving from side to side, and when you put the star scope on it, it sort of has a hollow center, a dark center. It's like the pupil of an eye looking at you, winking. And the flash is so bright to the star scope that, it almost burns your eye.

Halt and his men followed the light through the woods, crossing a farmer's field and stumbling through a small brook.

Halt later recalled: "As we moved out of the forest, we noticed three objects in the sky. The objects in the sky were moving about, sharp angular movements, very high speed. I kept getting on the radio and calling the command post. I wanted to know if they were finding anything on the radarscope. One of the objects was sending down beams, beams of light, beams of energy, I'm not sure what they were. At that same time I could hear on the radio, voices talking about the beams coming down on the base."

Then Halt saw a beam of light cut the night directly in front of him. That's when his skepticism disappeared for good.

He and his men chased the lights for more than an hour but to no avail. They finally left the forest around 3 A.M. But even after their departure, strange lights were still being reported above RAF Woodbridge.

The next morning, representatives from U.S. intelligence agencies started showing up at Bentwaters and Woodbridge.

Oddly (or maybe not), just about anyone who'd actually seen the UFOs in the woods was *not* questioned by the spooks. This included Lieutenant Colonel Halt, who was particularly marginalized. It is at this point that many ufologists contend the inevitable cover-up of the Rendlesham events began.

Still, whatever happened, there is no denying the episode had a significant effect on some of the men involved. For instance, soon after the incident Sergeant Penniston requested a transfer; the sighting had affected him adversely. On the other hand, John Burroughs, his partner in the woods that first night, stayed out in the forest for days afterward, waiting for the UFO to return.

Lieutenant Colonel Halt even sent blankets and food out to the airman during his vigil, but Burroughs refused to use them.

* * *

Once the Cold War ended, RAF Woodbridge and RAF Bentwaters were closed. Bentwaters was turned into a business park. Woodbridge is used today by the British army for training exercises.

The Rendlesham Forest itself was all but destroyed during England's "Great Storm of 1987." Since then many of the damaged trees have been replanted, though one report stated that glass globules were found in soil taken from the clearing where the first object had been seen. The same report said the area was also free of microbial growth.

The Rendlesham case is still investigated by ufologists today.

PART EIGHT

The Gulf War and Beyond

19

War in the
Garden of Eden

Operation Desert Shield

While the area around the Tigris and Euphrates rivers—
ancient Babylonia and now present-day Iraq—is considered
to be the cradle of civilization, the actual history of the
place is one of violence and war.

The Babylonian creation myth is a story of one god being
dismembered by another, the remains scattered across the
cosmos to form the universe. Ancient Sumerian legends
abound, with winged monsters battling each other above the
clouds before crashing to Earth. The first recorded war in
human history was fought in Mesopotamia around 3200
B.C. In fact, so many wars have been fought in the area over
the millennia, even historians can lose count.

If the ancient Achaemenian prophecy that says the world
will come to an end when Satan throws a comet at the earth

proves true, chances are good that comet will come down somewhere near the Persian Gulf.

It's no surprise, then, that soon after August 2, 1990, the day Saddam Hussein, then dictatorial ruler of Iraq, ordered his troops to invade the neighboring Persian Gulf country of Kuwait, strange things began showing up in the skies over the troubled Middle East.

Saddam's invasion was a grab for oil. In response, the United States and its allies began an enormous military buildup called Operation Desert Shield, its purpose being the eventual ejection of Saddam's troops from Kuwait.

So, as men and material from multiple countries poured into bases throughout the Middle East, the sight of all kinds of advanced, high-tech machines flying overhead became commonplace. But clearly some sightings did not fit the description of any known aircraft.

For instance, according to a report by the National UFO Reporting Center at www.nuforc.org, on a clear evening in September 1990, just weeks after Saddam's invasion, a U.S. Air Force advance unit working in the desert near Cairo, Egypt, had a very strange experience.

The seventy-member group was constructing a MASH facility and a fueling base in preparation for coming hostilities against Iraq. The group had finished work for the day and was heading back to their quarters when they were suddenly aware of a formation of pale orange objects flying high overhead. Aligned in a pair of parallel chevrons, as if forming a huge W, there were at least one hundred UFOs in the formation moving across the night sky.

Initially, the objects were traveling from the southeast to the northwest. But as the puzzled air force recruits looked on, the entire formation abruptly changed direction and began flying due north. In all, the phenomenon was visible for more than a half hour.

The next day the air force learned there had been no Egyptian or U.S. military aircraft overhead that night. In fact, no air traffic, military or commercial, had been scheduled for that airspace at all.

The sighting, so clearly reminiscent of Sergeant Stephen Brickner's famous Tulagi episode of World War II, was never explained.

According to a story on unsolvedmysteries.com, in November 1990, two months before hostilities broke out in the Gulf, four soldiers on guard duty at a U.S. Army compound in Al-Jubail, Saudi Arabia, saw a bright, blue white object traveling across the sky.

They judged it to be about 25,000 feet high—and surprisingly it made no sound. It flew slowly at first, following a seemingly random course that left a zigzag light trail overhead. After watching it for a short while, the soldiers saw it suddenly accelerate on a straight course and disappear in less than a second.

Around the same time, several marines also deployed in the area saw a similar object moving across the night sky. It too vanished in an instant.

Again, what surprised them was that they heard no sound. Otherwise, they would have thought they were looking at a helicopter.

* * *

Later the same month, a resident of Kerak, Jordan, was watching some storm clouds roll in from the Red Sea. The witness noticed one cloud was darker and at a lower altitude than the others; this cloud also seemed to be traveling at right angles to the rest.

This made no sense—but it got even stranger. As the witness watched in astonishment, the odd cloud separated itself from the rest of the cloud bank and flew directly overhead.

Within this strange cloud, the witness saw an oval object, metallic and silver gold in color. It was at least 100 feet long and had rapidly flashing red lights on it. The witness sensed that it was emitting a vibration, but there was no noise.

This object seemed to be heading toward Israel—not a good thing in a region that was well within range of Iraq's much-feared Scud missiles.

The witness continued watching the UFO until it faded over the horizon, its exact destination unknown.

One night in December 1990, crewmen aboard the aircraft carrier USS *John F. Kennedy* were preparing for action in the Persian Gulf.

Suddenly, a very bright, greenish yellow UFO appeared in the sky high over the massive aircraft carrier. The oval-shaped object remained stationary for almost a minute, as though it was spying on the huge ship.

Then the amazed crew saw what looked like an opening in the fabric of space. It drew the UFO into it, then closed instantly behind the object.

* * *

Another story found on the Web claimed that on January 15, 1991, just two days before the start of the war, a large number of U.S. soldiers saw a UFO over their camp in Saudi Arabia.

The object was oblong and bluish green in color. But it was its size that was so astonishing. Witnesses said the UFO was at least a quarter mile long and almost 1,000 feet wide. Gigantic by any standard of measurement.

The UFO appeared very suddenly and hovered silently over the troops for a long period of time. Then it eventually rose up and disappeared into the stars.

Many soldiers took pictures of the strange object, but the next day, witnesses said, military security people arrived at the camp and confiscated all the troopers' film.

Operation Desert Storm

The Gulf War began on January 17, 1991.

Code-named Operation Desert Storm, the opening shots were fired when President George H. W. Bush gave the go-ahead for a massive air strike on Iraq.

A story on nuforc.com tells of a startling incident that happened just after Bush's order. At 2:46 A.M. on that first day, a formation of four army MH-60 Black Hawk helicopters was making its way toward Iraq's border with Kuwait. Through his night vision goggles, the lead pilot spotted what he assumed was an F-117 "Stealth Fighter" approaching the formation at an altitude of just 1,000 feet.

This was odd. The premission briefing the copter pilots

had received made it clear there were not supposed to be any U.S. fighter aircraft in their area of operations. So what was this?

The object came within a quarter mile of the Black Hawks then slowed to a speed well below that of an F-117. At that point the chopper pilots knew this was not a Stealth Fighter.

The object turned sharply to the north, revealing a size of more than 80 feet long—far bigger than that of an F-117. It showed no lights and was not emitting any heat.

At that point, the object disappeared. When the team returned to base after completing their mission, the lead pilot asked flight operations if any fighters had been in their area of operations.

The response confirmed the earlier information: No other aircraft had flown anywhere near the Black Hawks at any time during their mission.

In March 1991, shortly after most hostilities had ceased, two American soldiers in the desert about 50 miles from the Euphrates River spotted something odd in the sky.

According to the story on UFOcasebook.com, it was after midnight, and the soldiers were on guard duty, looking out for any die-hard Iraqis who might want to attack their bivouacked army unit. As it was, the unit was only partially hidden by a couple of sand dunes, so everyone was on alert. Still, as all of the Coalition bombing had ended the day before, for the first time in a long while, the night was actually quiet.

Suddenly, the two soldiers spotted a greenish ball of light high in the sky. It moved very slowly, pulsating at times, heading for the horizon. The soldiers had no idea what it was.

Moments later, their sergeant happened upon the scene. They pointed out the UFO to him, but he had no idea what it was, either. The soldiers radioed their headquarters to see if any fighter jets or commercial flights would be flying over their position. They were told no.

Still watching the UFO, the men were again astonished when the object suddenly accelerated to tremendous speed. When that happened, everything for miles around was lit up in the same greenish light. One soldier compared it to a hundred cars suddenly turning on their headlights at once. And with that, the object was over the horizon and gone.

The soldiers called their headquarters to see if any Scud missiles had been fired or if there had been any reports of planes crashing. But they were told nothing unusual had happened that night.

The next morning, about two hundred Iraqi soldiers surrendered to the American unit, eagerly giving up their weapons in the process.

Whether the Iraqis had also seen the UFO, and whether it had an effect on their surrender, was not known.

Another incident after the end of hostilities happened in the northern city of Zahko, Iraq.

According to a story found on www.rense.com a unit of American paratroopers had set up camp in a partially blasted-out building near the center of the city. The paratroopers would frequently sleep on the roof of this building, as it was cooler in the hot Iraqi nights.

One such night, a paratrooper was looking for satellites

going over in the clear, starry sky, when he noticed a strange light. He thought he'd found a satellite at first, but then, inexplicably, whatever it was suddenly stopped in midorbit. It stayed motionless for a few moments, then resumed moving again.

Convinced that his eyes were playing tricks on him, the paratrooper mentioned it to one of his fellow soldiers. He asked him to watch the object as well. And at first this soldier thought it was a satellite, too—until it stopped in midflight again.

For the next few minutes, the two soldiers watched the object, as it would move north, stop for a few moments, then resume crossing the sky. Even stranger, anytime the object would stop, the sky around it would almost explode in brightness, the object getting brighter than the brightest star in the sky, before becoming so dim, it would almost disappear.

The first trooper finally yelled to the others in his unit, and soon up to two dozen paratroopers were watching as the object went through a series of elaborate maneuvers including slow deliberate circles and figure eights.

The sighting ended when the object stopped in the middle of a figure eight, hung motionless for a moment and then rocketed off to the northeast faster, as one witness put it, than the human eye could keep up with it.

When it comes to UFO sightings in wartime, this handful of eyewitness accounts above doesn't seem any less plausible than any other episodes presented so far.

But a trio of other incidents, though of dubious authenticity, persist when it comes to UFO lore, the first Gulf War and beyond.

One maintains that U.S Navy ships patrolling the Persian Gulf during the war shot down a UFO. This supposedly highly classified shoot down happened during daylight hours on January 24, 1991, just a week after the hostilities had begun.

As the story goes, the unidentified flying object was first picked up on radar by a host of navy ships supporting the allied combat operations in the upper gulf. According to its radar tracks, the object was flying in a very bizarre manner and outside the realm of even the most high-tech Coalition warplane. Crews of the ships involved quickly acquired the object visually, describing it as saucer shaped, chromium plated and emitting a high-pitched piercing sound.

The object flew close to a group of American ships, including the USS *Wisconsin*, USS *England* and USS *O'Brien*. Then it buzzed a pair of British frigates, the HMS *Battleaxe* and HMS *Jupiter*, as well.

All five vessels fired on the object, nearly expending their ammunition before the combined barrage had any effect. The object was finally hit and was seen going down into the gulf.

But there are no reports of any wreckage ever being found.

The second incident involves an F-16 fighter jet dogfighting and then shooting down a UFO over Saudi Arabia at the height of the war.

The principal purveyor of this episode is a shadowy

Russian colonel worthy of a James Bond novel. The Russian officer just happened to be in Riyadh, the capital of Saudi Arabia, when the shoot-down episode took place. He claimed to be one of the first people to know the location of the UFO's crash site, which was deep in the Saudi desert, some 250 miles northeast of Riyadh.

Saudi radar technicians told the Russian officer the details of the air battle. Four U.S. Air Force F-16s were on a mission to Baghdad when an unidentified blip appeared on their radar screens. As the Saudi technicians watched, one of the F-16s left the formation and started chasing the UFO. The UFO changed directions in an attempt to escape, but the F-16 continued in pursuit. The UFO then apparently fired a weapon at the F-16 but missed. The F-16 returned fire with two missiles—and both hit the craft. The UFO went down in flames.

The Saudis said no one was seen ejecting from the stricken craft. But even though helicopters scoured the area over the crash site, no bodies or survivors were found.

The Russian colonel said the United States immediately tried to cover up the incident, saying it never happened. But upon reaching the crash site and seeing the wreckage for himself, the Russian knew it was not from any known earthly aircraft. He estimated about one third of the object had been destroyed by the American missiles, leaving the rest scattered on the desert floor.

The colonel described the downed craft as having been circular and built of some unrecognizable material. It was about 15 feet long and, judging by the seats within, built for someone, or *something*, of small stature. The Russian says he saw instruments, machinery and other things that defied description. This included markings on the instrument panels that were written in some indecipherable language. The Saudis who accompanied him to the crash site were so frightened by the strange debris, and what it might mean, they requested that American investigators come to the crash site immediately.

When the U.S. military finally arrived, the colonel said he and his men were immediately ordered out of the area. They were eventually flown back to Riyadh.

The colonel was reported to have said: "There were things the Americans didn't want us to see."

And though his men were able to surreptitiously take photographs of the UFO's wreckage, the next day, the colonel was ordered by authorities from his own country to turn over all photos of the crash site to them.

The colonel said he learned later that the U.S. Army eventually gathered up the crash debris, put it into crates and flew it all back to the United States.

The third story having to do with UFOs and warfare in the Persian Gulf region also has surprising resiliency—and brings the whole story right up to the present day. What's more, it's also connected to the same mysterious Russian colonel.

This account always seems to start out with the same question: Did Saddam Hussein at one time possess a UFO?

This, in turn, leads to two more questions: Did Saddam's regime have its own top secret version of Area 51? And if so, was this where the elusive WMD, the unfound weapons of mass destruction that led to the 2003 U.S. invasion of Iraq, were actually stored?

Even before that massive assault against Saddam began,

there were persistent reports that the dictator had come into possession of a damaged UFO, possibly shot down either during the 1991 war, or more likely around 1998, while the U.S. military was enforcing a strict no-fly zone over Iraq.

That particular scenario starts on December 16, 1998, when a video clip, said to have aired on CNN, appeared to show a UFO flying over Baghdad. The object was seen trying to avoid antiaircraft fire being shot at it by Saddam's forces.

At the time it was assumed this was just another UFO sighting, one of dozens that take place around the world every day. But then rumors started bubbling up that maybe the UFO was actually hit by the AA fire, shot down and recovered by Saddam's military.

As the story went, the UFO, or pieces of it, were then taken to Iraq's version of Area 51, a place known as Qalaat-e-Julundi. Once there, Saddam had his weapons experts reverse engineer the alien technology, and from *that*, create some mind boggling WMD.

So, was *this* fantastic weapons cache what the United States was secretly after all along? Was this the elusive WMD?

Even scientists within Iraq didn't totally discount this theory. Some even took it one step further by claiming that extraterrestrials who'd survived the UFO crash had been living in the modern Babylonia under Saddam's protection.

One scientist was quoted before the 2003 invasion as saying: "It is rumored at a market in Sulaimaniya, to the south of Zarzi, that aliens are Saddam's guests. Where do they stay? People mention some underground base at the old stronghold Qalaat-e-Julundi. It is practically impossible to penetrate into it. The citadel stands on a hill surrounded with vertical precipices on three sides; the precipices plunge down to the Little Zab River. It is said that Saddam lets aliens stay there."

Then the story gets even better.

"Saddam gave the aliens sanctuary, so that they couldn't be captured by the Americans," the scientist claimed. "Nobody can reach the citadel Qalaat-e-Julundi at night. They say that the aliens created 'watchdogs' for Saddam. The aliens took ordinary desert scorpions and used their bio-engineering to grow them to giant size. Scorpions of a cow-size! They are wonderful watchdogs: they blend in with the desert, swiftly and silently move on their warm-blooded prey for a decisive attack. Luckless intruders just hear some strange sound from behind, then a pincer crushes their necks, another pincer crushes their legs. Death comes almost immediately."

It's a crazy tale—and possibly created solely to keep the highly superstitious Iraqis away from a legitimate military installation located in the old fortress of Qalaat-e-Julundi.

But what's interesting about this account is that much of it, along with the mysterious Russian colonel's UFO shootdown story, was reported, quotes included, in *Pravda*, the onetime official newspaper of the Soviet Union.

And while the *Pravda* of the old Moscow regime doesn't exist now as it did then, it is still a media outlet in Russia. A bit sensationalistic, but still highly read.

As one Russian journalist who didn't want to give his name explained to us: "*Pravda* today is sort of 'yellowish.' They don't have any correspondents' network or stringers. They are sensation hunters and usually compile second-hand news from the Internet.

"However, that does not mean what they write about is not true."

20

The Grand Puzzle

Among his fellow UFO researchers, the late Richard Hall was known as the "Dean of Ufology."

Best described as a critical-minded proponent, his 1964 book *The UFO Evidence* is considered one of the best ever written on the subject. Simply put, Hall believed that UFOs were extraterrestrial and that the U.S. military was deceiving the American people when it came to what they knew about them.

According to his obituary, published in the *Washington Post,* in a 1966 paper, Hall wrote: "Ninety-seven percent of the nibbles a fisherman feels on his line may be caused by his line snagging on rocks or seaweed or by wave motion. But that doesn't prove there are no fish in the ocean."

These are more than just wise words for describing the UFO mystery; there are numbers that bear them out. By the time the U.S. Air Force officially closed Project Blue Book in 1969, it had collected reports on about 13,000 UFO sightings. At least 700 of them—a significant number—were labeled unexplained.

However, when factored in that much of the activity at Blue Book from 1952 onward was devoted to whitewashing UFO sightings, that 700 figure has got to be regarded as being very, very low.

More numbers. Polls in the United States say forty million people have either seen a UFO themselves or know someone who has. *Eighty* million U.S. citizens believe Earth has been visited by extraterrestrials.

Several thousand UFO sightings are reported each year. Several *hundred* thousand have been documented over the past half century or so.

But because only a fraction of people who actually see a UFO report it, this means the actual number of UFO sightings since the early 1950s is in the *millions*.

Something is happening. True, there's a lot of clutter and a lot of noise. But all these sightings cannot be illusions, birds, airplanes, weather balloons, reentry vehicles or the planet Venus. And all it takes is for one of them to be true—because then, in a way, they *all* become true.

But how do we get to the truth?

The UFO enigma is so important that it demands to be placed in the hands of objective, apolitical, purely scientific-minded people whose goal must be to simply tell us what we've been seeing all these years. What *are* these things that have been flying around our skies, watching our wars, tampering with our doomsday weapons, and quite possibly altering the course of human events by, for example, appearing in the sky in the shape of a cross?

More than $10 billion was spent to build the Large Hadron Collider in Switzerland in an effort to re-create the first few microseconds of the Big Bang. NASA has spent billions on satellites, space probes and earthbound listening stations, all in its search for the secrets of the universe and the possibility of life different than ours among the stars. One would think the same type of earnestness, dedication and curiosity would have been directed to solving the question of UFOs.

Instead, the job was given to the U.S. military—and considering the results, or the lack of them, that might go down as one of the worst decisions in history.

We were fooled at first. When the U.S. Air Force set up Project Blue Book in 1951, people were led to believe it would be a vast scientific institute like Fermilab, or Los Alamos, or Oak Ridge, Tennessee. In reality, it was never more than one office and four people, two of whom were secretaries, all under orders to lay low and not to make waves.

More numbers—and this time they have dollar signs attached to them. During the 1950s, the Pentagon spent hundreds of billions of dollars on defense. Yet at one point, Captain Ruppelt's Blue Book was so impoverished it didn't have enough money to even read over all the sighting reports it was taking in.

The Pentagon cheapened out when it came to studying UFOs. The institution that historically overspends on *everything* chose to nickel-and-dime this very important matter. Why? There's only one answer. They did it because they never intended to do a good job in the first place. In fact, the goal all along was to do the worst job possible.

As J. Allen Hynek said in 1972 in *Fate* magazine: "It became patently clear to me as the years passed that no Blue Book case had been given the 'FBI treatment.' That is, no case was followed through until every possible clue or bit of evidence was obtained, as is standard procedure in kidnapping, narcotics rings and bank robbery cases.

"Quite the opposite attitude was taken by Blue Book. When a case did appear to have a likely misperception explanation (and hence should have been excluded from further UFO investigative effort) Blue Book often spared little effort in phone calls, interrogations, etc., in order to pin it down to a planet, a refueling mission, or some other natural occurrence. Thus they set their dogs to catching simple chicken thieves but ignored potentially far more important prey."

The supreme irony is that finding out what UFOs are might not be that hard. UFOs are not like quirks, quarks and quacks. They are not as elusive as the Higgs boson particle. They are not things that one has to build a $10 billion supercollider to take snapshots of, pictures that last for one billionth of one trillionth of a second before they disappear.

Just the opposite. UFOs are all around us. There's a reason that millions have been reported over the years. The misconception is that UFOs don't want us to see them, but the evidence indicates the reverse is true.

The scareships gliding over the British landscape, their searchlights turned up to high? The ghost planes waking up the frozen Scandinavian tundra, their engines roaring, *their* searchlights also ablaze? The foo fighters tagging along on 800-plane bombing raids? The ghost rockets flying by the hundreds every day? Huge saucers over Korea? A dozen saucers over the White House?

These are not the actions of an entity that is hiding or being secretive. We might not know *what* they are, but it's clear they have no problem letting us know that they are here. That is the grand puzzle.

But every puzzle has a solution. So, when will the UFO question finally be solved?

Stan Gordon, the man who has dutifully kept the Kecksburg mystery alive all these years, told us in an interview: "When the 'powers that be' make the decision, or when circumstances occur that can't be hidden away."

When we asked Richard Haines, the NASA expert who turned his talents to studying UFOs, the same question, he went right to the point. "We'll know when 'they' want us to know."

Keith Chester, who'll be forever known as the man who finally told the whole foo fighters story, told us: "It will take undeniable evidence of extraterrestrial visitation for the whole world to witness for this riddle to be truly solved."

Jerome Clark, aforementioned author of numerous UFO articles and books, took a more existential view:

"Science has largely ignored the UFO phenomenon," he told us. "Leaving the issue to military agencies, civilian researchers, and debunkers. The UFO problem is not inherently unsolvable, however, and while sometimes science is slow to take up complicated, troublesome issues, it does get there eventually. I believe that by the middle of the 21st century learned people will start to look into this phenomenon and finally make up for the lost opportunity we had back in 1948."

We hope Clark is right. We also hope he's off his time-table a bit and that we get some answers before 2050.

Most important, though, when the serious study of UFOs begins again, no matter who champions it, who pushes for it, or who pays for it—we hope, this time, they don't put the U.S. military in charge.

BIBLIOGRAPHY

The following books, articles and websites were invaluable to me while writing this book. I urge all to look into the UFO question more deeply by reading these and other works.

Chester, Keith. *Strange Company: Military Encounters with UFOS in WWII.* Anomalist Books. San Antonio. 2007.

Clark, Jerome. *Strange Skies: Pilot Encounters with UFOs.* Citadel Press. New York. 2003.

Clark, Jerome; Farish, Lucius. Article, "The Mysterious 'Foo Fighters' of World War II," in 1977 UFO Annual.

Clark, Jerome. *The UFO Encyclopedia, Second Edition: The Phenomenon from the Beginning.* Two volumes. Omnigraphics. Detroit. 1998.

Cooper, Gordon; Henderson, Bruce. *Leap of Faith.* HarperTorch. New York. 2000.

Good, Timothy. *Need To Know: UFOs, the Military, and Intelligence.* Pegasus Books. New York. 2007.

Hall, Richard, H. (ed.) *The National Investigations Committee on Aerial Phenomena (NICAP) The UFO Evidence.* Barnes and Noble Books. New York. 1964.

BIBLIOGRAPHY

Hastings, Robert. *UFOs and Nukes: Extraordinary Encounters at Nuclear Weapons Sites*. Authorhouse. Bloomington. 2008.

Kean, Leslie. *UFOs: Generals, Pilots, and Government Officials Go on the Record*. Harmony Books. New York. 2010.

Keyhoe, Donald E. *Flying Saucers: Top Secret*. G. P. Putnam's Sons. New York. 1960.

Pflock, Karl, T. *Roswell: Inconvenient Facts and the Will to Believe*. Prometheus Books. Amherst. 2001.

Randle, Kevin, D. *Invasion Washington: UFOs Over the Capitol*. Harper-Torch, New York. 2001.

Ruppelt, Edward, J. *The Report on Unidentified Flying Objects*. Filiquarian Publishing.

Vallee, Jacques and Janine. *Challenge to Science: The UFO Enigma*. Ballantine Books. New York. 1966.

Vallee, Jacques. *Anatomy of a Phenomenon: UFOs in Space*. Ballantine Books. New York. 1965.

Wyatt, John, "The *Hobart* Incident," AUFORN Special Report, Issue 34, April 2003.

www.colinandrews.net/UFO-MiltonTorres.html

www.mtpioneer.com/March-Malstrom-UFOs.html

www.nickpope.net/rendlesham-forest.htm

www.nuforc.org

www.ufocasebook.com

www.ufoevidence.org

tvufo.tripod.com/id116.html

www.allsupernatural.net/aliens/ufo/story/136/ufo-attack-n-vietnam-1968/

www.alien-ufos.com/ufo-alien-discussions/22198-ufo-reports-during-vietnam-war.html

files.abovetopsecret.com/images/member/e3c51170ec1a.jpg

www.unsolvedmysteries.com/default.asp?action=ndate